best hikes with dogs

GEORGIA & SOUTH CAROLINA

best hikes with dogs

GEORGIA & SOUTH CAROLINA

**Steve Goodrich &
Ashley Goodrich**

THE MOUNTAINEERS BOOKS

Dedication

To Rebel, our yellow lab and constant hiking companion. May you wander the trails forever, our friend.

THE MOUNTAINEERS BOOKS
is the nonprofit publishing arm of The Mountaineers Club, an organization founded in 1906 and dedicated to the exploration, preservation, and enjoyment of outdoor and wilderness areas.

1001 SW Klickitat Way, Suite 201, Seattle, WA 98134

First edition, 2007

Manufactured in the United States of America

Copy Editor: Jane Crosen
Cover and Book Design: The Mountaineers Books
Layout: Marge Mueller, Gray Mouse Graphics
Cartographer: Jim Miller, Fenanna Design
Photographer: All photos are by Steve Goodrich except photos on pages 151, 153, 155, and 157 are by Roger Cardoc, and on pages 16 and 82 are by Rob Schwartz.

Cover photograph: *The authors' dog, Rebel, anxiously awaits an exciting afternoon on the trail.*
Frontispiece: *Rebel before a backpacking trip in North Georgia*

Maps shown in this book were produced using National Geographic's TOPO! software. For more information, go to *www.nationalgeographic.com/topo*.

Library of Congress Cataloging-in-Publication Data
Goodrich, Steve.
 Best hikes with dogs. Georgia & South Carolina / Steve and Ashley Goodrich.—1st ed.
         p.   cm.
 Includes bibliographical references and index.
 ISBN 0-89886-817-3 (ppb : alk. paper)
 1. Hiking with dogs—Georgia—Guidebooks. 2. Trails—Georgia—Guidebooks.
 3. Georgia—Guidebooks. 4. Hiking with dogs—South Carolina—Guidebooks.
 5. Trails—South Carolina—Guidebooks. 6. South Carolina—Guidebooks.
 I. Goodrich, Ashley. II. Title.
 SF427.455.G66 2007
 796.5109758—dc22
                     2006030379

CONTENTS

Part 1: Hiking with Your Dog

Part 2: Georgia

Northern Georgia

Central/Southern Georgia

Part 3: South Carolina

Northwestern South Carolina

Northern/Central South Carolina

Southern South Carolina

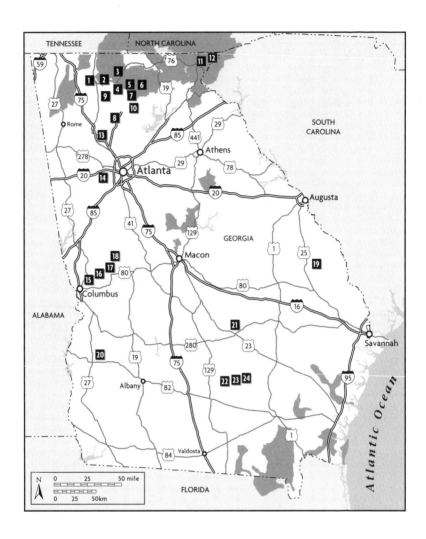

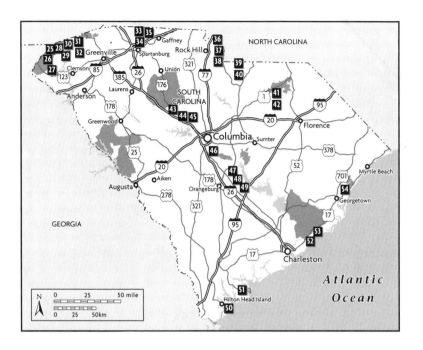

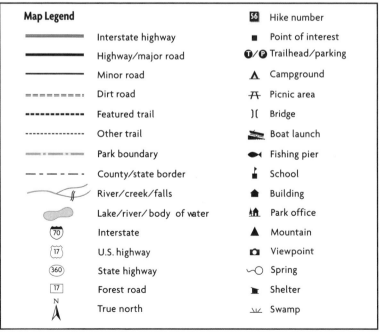

Map Legend

═══════	Interstate highway
▬▬▬▬▬	Highway/major road
▬▬▬▬▬	Minor road
=========	Dirt road
-------------	Featured trail
---------------	Other trail
▬ · ▬ · ▬	Park boundary
— - — - —	County/state border
⌒⌒⌿⌿	River/creek/falls
▬	Lake/river/ body of water
(70)	Interstate
(17)	U.S. highway
(360)	State highway
[17]	Forest road
N ⋏	True north

56	Hike number
■	Point of interest
❶/ℙ	Trailhead/parking
▲	Campground
🕱	Picnic area
)(	Bridge
⛵	Boat launch
🐟	Fishing pier
🏴	School
⬟	Building
🏛	Park office
▲	Mountain
📷	Viewpoint
⌒○	Spring
▰	Shelter
⟱	Swamp

HIKE SUMMARY TABLE

Hike	5 miles (or less)	Mountains	Water to splash in	Waterfall view	Swamp/marshland	Backcountry campsite	Great for smaller or older dogs	Great for fit dogs	Loop hike
1. Conasauga River	●		●			●			
2. Toccoa River		●	●			●		●	
3. Green Mountain	●	●					●		●
4. Ramrock Mountain	●	●				●	●		
5. Coosa Bald		●		●		●		●	●
6. Bear Hair Gap Trail	●			●			●	●	●
7. Blood Mountain		●				●		●	●
8. Frosty Mountain		●				●		●	●
9. Springer Mountain	●	●				●	●		●
10. DeSoto Falls	●			●		●			
11. Black Rock Mountain	●	●		●			●		●
12. Rabun Bald		●		●		●	●		
13. Lake Allatoona			●						●
14. Sweetwater Creek	●		●	●			●		●
15. Buzzard Roost			●			●	●	●	●
16. Lil' Butt Knob						●	●	●	●
17. Sunset Rock						●	●	●	●
18. The Wolfden					●	●			●
19. Beaver Trail	●		●				●		●
20. Providence Canyon						●			●
21. Oak Ridge Trail	●				●		●		●
22. Gopher Loop Trail	●		●		●		●		●
23. West River Swamp Trail	●		●		●	●			
24. East River Swamp Trail	●		●		●	●			
25. Ellicott Rock			●			●			
26. King Creek Falls	●		●	●		●	●		
27. Long Mountain		●		●		●			

Hike	5 miles (or less)	Mountains	Water to splash in	Waterfall view	Swamp/marshland	Backcountry campsite	Great for smaller or older dogs	Great for fit dogs	Loop hike
28. Lick Log Creek Falls			•	•		•			
29. Yellow Branch Falls	•	•		•			•		
30. Matthews Creek		•	•	•		•			•
31. Middle Saluda River			•	•		•			
32. Raven Cliff Falls	•	•		•		•	•		
33. Battlefield Trail	•						•		•
34. Browns Mountain		•				•		•	•
35. Kings Mountain Nature Trail	•						•		•
36. Lake Haigler	•		•				•		•
37. Springfield Trail	•						•		•
38. Landsford Canal	•		•				•		
39. Garden of the Waxhaws	•		•				•		•
40. Crawford Hiking Trail	•						•		•
41. Cheraw Nature Trail	•						•		•
42. Turkey Oak Trail	•						•		•
43. Stewardship Trail	•		•				•		•
44. Learning Trail	•						•		•
45. Midlands Mountain Trail	•		•					•	•
46. Oakridge and Kingsnake Trail	•		•		•		•		•
47. Oak Pinolley Trail	•		•		•		•		•
48. Santee Bike/Hike Trail					•				•
49. Limestone Nature Trail	•				•		•		•
50. Jarvis Creek Park	•		•				•		•
51. Hunting Island Trail			•		•		•		•
52. I'on Swamp	•				•		•		•
53. Sewee Shell Mound	•		•		•		•		•
54. Huntington Beach	•		•		•		•		•

ACKNOWLEDGMENTS

In writing this guidebook, there were a host of federal, state, and city officials who provided valuable guidance and feedback on the text and trail maps in the following pages. We have done our best to recognize them for their assistance and to pay tribute to our friends and trail companions who have contributed in some way to this book. Thanks to all of you, and may this guidebook serve you well in the wilderness of Georgia and South Carolina:

Federal, State, and City Officials
Jackie Clay (General Coffee State Park), Alessandra Delfico (Hilton Head Island), Bill Giles (Magnolia Springs State Park), Wade Huffman (Magnolia Springs State Park), Bob Klink (Hilton Head Island), David Kuykendall (Chattahoochee National Forest: Brasstown Ranger District), Anthony Lampros (Black Rock Mountain State Park), Brenda Magers (Huntington Beach State Park), Laura Maxley (Hilton Head Island), Drew McCarley (Chattahoochee National Forest: Armuchee/Cohutta Ranger District), Joe Penale (Hilton Head Island), Fran Rametta (Congaree Swamp National Park), Bill Steele (Anne Springs Close Greenway), Don Scarbrough (Sweetwater Creek State Conservation Park), Brad Wise (Santee State Park).

Family, Friends, and Trail Companions
Sheryl "The Weight" Allen, Kirk "SoulGlo" Andrews, Jeff "Smoky" Atkinson, Mike "The Cowboy" Baldwin, Robb and Tammie "Tamalama" Beatty, James Bland, Beth "Firecracker" Bernardo, Bill "Mackie" Blaylock, Liz Boulware, Phillip "Black Crowe" Boyd, Charlie "The Operator" Brady, Katie "Wild Turkey" Brady, Will "Wicked Ale" Brewer, Harry Bruen, Matt "Boyz In The Wood" Brunn, Jim "Country Club" Bunting, Roger "The Camel" Cardoe, Elizabeth "Sister" Cobb, Steve "White Lightening" Cobb, Micheal "Waterdog" Crook, Christianne "CC" Curran, Pratt "Wagonhammer" Davis, Joe DeLisle, Gardiner "Maineac" Doughty, David Ewing, Angela "Artic Fox" Funicello, Joe "The Shiek" Fess, Robert "Freedog" Freedman, Jeff "The Joker" Gibson, David "Squeezebox" Gibson, Robbie "The Gomite" Gomez, Dick and Mary Goodrich, John Grimes, Alison "ALE" Hackney, Kevin "The Seeker" Hicks, Nikki "Tired Dogs" Hinds, Douglas "DooRag" Jones, Chris "Sikle" Kasischke, Alan "The Senator" Kennedy, Mike "Jive Turkey" Kennedy, Ken "The Weasel" Knight, Ron

Lee, Stephen "Troubadour" Martin, Sloane Mayberry, David McKinney, Russ and Terry Menard (Slowly And Surely), Darrin "Oskie" Milne, Greg "Eveready AT92" Moehlich, Morgan "Monodeep" Mitra, Kristin Mitra, Andy "CA" Morrison, Jeff Nause, William and Barb O'Neil (Walking Stick and Laughing Bird), Rob "Black Sunshine" Pangle, Derek "Boyz In The Wood" Porter, "Laid Back Sue" Robertson, Matt "Yukon Matt" Russell, Katherine "Pocohontas" Schuler, Rob "The Rooster" Schwartz, Glenn "The Helmet" Schuffenhaeur, Alec Sedki, Nebil and Marlo Sedki, Susan "Doughgirl" Schuffenhaeur, Jimmy "Slawdog" Slate, Brooke "Babbles" Smith, Steve "The Ox" Snyder, Keith "Stuffsack" Trevett, Lee Tucker, Bob And Diane Wheelock (Motor City Ramblers), David "Nomad" Young, John "The Kidd" Zedd.

Major, a golden retriever owned by Steve and Shana Snyder, dries off after a swim in the Conasauga River.

PREFACE

There is no better time for a dog than a day spent with his/her owner experiencing the sights, smells, tastes, and sounds of the great outdoors. There is something primeval about the wilderness, and both man and dog know it. What calls us back again and again is an opportunity to share the experience with our trail hound—our best friend and constant companion.

If your dog is like ours, he shakes with energy as soon as you pull into the trailhead. Rain or shine, our four-legged friend is always ready—eager to get off the couch, out of the house, and hit the trail. He rarely complains, will swim any stream, stop at any vista, and go any distance. Walk with him, play with him, care for him, and he'll gladly curl up beside you at the campfire—snoring in your ear throughout the night. We have hiked many miles with our canine friend and taken him on countless day and overnight trips. Sometimes we carry packs, and other times we enjoy the freedom of traveling light.

This book is written for dog-lovers like us who enjoy the wilderness and want to share the experience with their pet. Our hope is that it guides you through many enjoyable moments in the backcountry and that you cherish the experience as much as we do.

PART 1

Hiking with Your Dog

Getting Ready

In this guidebook, every attempt is made to provide the most accurate data possible, but weather and trail conditions can change and without notice. So consider your brain the most valuable resource that you have while hiking in the backcountry. Some common hazards are outlined later in "On the Trail," and it is best to review each scenario and prepare before you head into the wilderness. Preparation is the key to a successful and enjoyable experience on the trail—so take it seriously.

When and Where to Go

The Southeastern United States is blessed with a variety of terrain and trail conditions for hikers and their dogs. The northern sections of Georgia and northwestern South Carolina have rolling hills and mountains

Max, a beagle owned by Rob and Mary Schwartz, on the trail in North Georgia

rising to over 4000 feet. The coastal areas have flat, fertile lowlands that include both dark and soggy swamps and sandy and pristine beaches. The goal of this guidebook is to provide hikers and their pets with at least a few trail options in each area and to make them convenient from any given point in Georgia and South Carolina. Ideally, you can wake up on a Saturday morning and drive to a trailhead within two hours. For this reason, we organized the book in five sections to make it easier to find a hike from any major geographical area—Northern Georgia, Central/Southern Georgia, Northwestern South Carolina, Northern/Central South Carolina, and Southern South Carolina:

North Georgia. The northern part of Georgia is characterized by the rolling hills of the Piedmont, which gradually increase in size from one to four thousand feet as one drives northward from Macon, through Atlanta, and into the North Georgia mountains. Brasstown Bald, located in northeastern corner of Georgia, is the highest point in the State at 4,784 feet, and hikers and backpackers are occasionally surprised by the winter snows that can blanket these high peaks during the winter season. These ranges include both the Blue Ridge Mountains to the northeast and the Appalachian Mountains to the north. Both are heavily forested with soft pines and hardwoods that sometimes open to rocky outcroppings and summits with spectacular views in all directions. Hiking trails are numerous in North Georgia, with many acres of national and state forest land to choose from for your day or overnight excursion. On average, these hikes are the longest, most remote, and most difficult in the book. So plan accordingly, and consider hiking the easy to moderate routes if you (or your pet) are new to the trail.

Central/South Georgia. The central and southern section of Georgia is comprised of the Atlantic and East Gulf coastal plains which are characterized by flat, sandy, and occasionally swampy conditions that offer hikers and backpackers some of the easiest terrain in the book. Hikers and backpackers are advised to avoid the hot and humid summer months in this region and to carry insect repellant year round. Many of the hikes in South Georgia are within the boundary of state parks, which means well-managed, user-friendly trails with amenities including campgrounds, restrooms, and picnic areas nearby.

Northwestern South Carolina. The Blue Ridge Mountains which run through the Northwestern corner of the State are smaller in size than their North Georgia counterparts, but still reach 3,554 feet in elevation at Sassafras Mountain, the highest point in South Carolina. Many trails in this book are selected from the streams and rivers that carve through the Blue Ridge, and include hikes along the Chattooga and Middle Saluda Rivers. These trails are the most remote in South Carolina and often traverse federal and state park land with easy access to swimming and fishing holes that are great to visit in the hot and humid summer months.

Northern/Central South Carolina. Locals commonly refer to this area as the Piedmont in South Carolina and it is characterized by gentle rolling hills that range from 400 to 1,400 feet in elevation. The trails in this region are clustered around Rock Hill and Columbia and are moderate in difficulty, with walks along lightly forested areas that occasionally circumvent a lake or follow the length of a river or stream. State Parks and Forests offer the majority of these trails with excellent amenities nearby.

Southern South Carolina. The Atlantic Coastal Plain covers two-thirds of the State of South Carolina and extends from the coast to 70 miles inland. It is very flat with numerous rivers and swamps draining toward the coast. Sand hills are common in the region, and geologists believe that it was underwater at some time in our past. Elevation change is minimal in this area, but hikers should not underestimate the difficulty in hiking the sandy beaches and swampy forests. Both are best avoided during the extreme heat of summer when insects are at their worst. National and state parks offer the bulk of hikes here, some of which are along the coast and offer a surprising amount of solitude.

Our goal in this book is to provide eight to twelve hikes in each geographic region and offer a dog-friendly hiking experience with a worthwhile destination on the route: a historic building, scenic view, cascading waterfalls, etc. Hiking times are based on a pace of no more than two miles per hour, which is the average speed for a backcountry hiker. We have listed the color of the blazes, the 2x6 inch vertical rectangles that mark the route, and have suggested a time for each adventure. In the summer months, seek out higher ground when possible where breezy and cooler conditions prevail. Avoid the coastal areas when the heat, humidity, and insects can take their toll on both you and your trail hound.

In the winter months, be prepared with extra clothing and watch the weather forecast carefully before you head out. The hiking trails are less traveled in the winter, offer more solitude, and provide more scenic views without the summer foliage. Another way to avoid the crowds is to go during the week—particularly in the state and national forests—which is an effective strategy year round. When possible, avoid the weekends, especially three-day weekends, and you will experience more solitude and have more freedom for your pet, who is likely quite eager to get off the leash.

Trail Management

The majority of the hikes in this book are managed by either a state park or the National Forest Service. Funding varies between agencies, so their facilities and trail conditions can be dramatically different depending on the management agency, their regulations, and their budgets. As a general rule, here is what to expect with each management group:

National parks. Most national parks require that dogs are on a leash at all times, and that the leash be no longer than six feet in length. Some in Georgia and South Carolina do not allow dogs at all—particularly the coastal national parks and wildlife refuges such as Cumberland Island. National parks typically have a visitor center, campground, picnic area, and tend to have well-maintained and well-marked backcountry hiking trails and campsites. Funding comes from federal tax dollars, and the national parks in the South are pretty heavily used with strict rules and regulations—particularly for dogs.

State parks. In general, the state parks in Georgia and South Carolina tend to be the best funded of the agencies and have the nicest facilities and amenities, which often include a visitor center, campground, and picnic area like the national parks. They generally offer trail maps at the visitor center. Most state parks require that dogs are on a leash at all times, and that the leash be no longer than six feet in length. Most rental cabins at the parks do not allow dogs, although they are usually permitted in the campgrounds. Trails in the state parks tend to be well maintained and well marked, with state funds supporting the efforts. The state parks in Georgia and South Carolina are pretty heavily used—especially the parks with large lakes—and they often have strict rules and regulations for dogs.

National forests. The national forests are the most dog-friendly of the wilderness management agencies. Most require that the pooch stay on a leash or under voice command, but they have fewer facilities and are not as heavily used as the national and state parks. Most of the hikes in the national forests do not have a convenient place nearby to get trail

Andy Morrison plays with his dog, Buddy, on the summit of Rabun Bald in North Georgia.

maps, so it is better to pick one up before leaving town. A subset of the national forests is the wilderness management areas. A WMA is an undeveloped federal land area under the jurisdiction of the National Forest Service, by definition a large tract of protected land with no improvements and no permanent human habitation. The Cohutta Wilderness in the Chattahoochee National Forest of Georgia is an example of a WMA. These areas often provide the most primitive conditions for the hiker and backpacker and the most opportunity for solitude.

State forests. Although there are many more acres of national forest land in Georgia and South Carolina, there is a surprising amount of state forest acreage that offers recreational activities for hikers and backpackers. State forests (like the Harbison State Forest in South Carolina) are usually more primitive than the state parks but are also more lenient with fewer restrictions. Funding for management and maintenance is provided by the state, and most state forests require that dogs are leashed or under voice command at all times. Call ahead for confirmation if the rules and restrictions are not stated in this book, or check the website: *www.state. sc.us/forest/recreat.htm*

Getting Your Dog Ready

Hiking and backpacking with your dog can be a very fun or extremely miserable experience, depending on your level of preparation. When dogs get a bad rap on the trail, it is usually the owner and not the pet who is the problem. For most people, a well-behaved and well-mannered pet is a pleasure to be around—particularly on a hiking trail. Unfortunately, not all owners keep them on a leash or under voice control, pick up after their pet, or raise a socialized dog that gets along well with other animals. For this reason, most of the state and national parks require that dogs are on a leash at all times. So it is your responsibility to follow the rules and regulations and make sure you always have a leash with you, wherever you hike.

Identification, License, and Vaccinations

The first step is to make sure that your dog has a collar with updated contact, license, and vaccination information (including rabies, bordatella, and heartworm). This sounds intuitive, but it is probably the last thing on your mind when you hit the trail. A few years ago, we were on an overnight backpacking trip at Caesars Head in South Carolina, and a dog wandered into our camp as we sat around the campfire in the evening. It had been lost for days, was very skinny, and immediately wolfed down what little food we had left. Our efforts to contact the owner were hindered by an outdated phone number on the dog's collar. A few days later, a park ranger tracked down the owner, just before it was scheduled for a trip to the pound. You get the point.

Since collars can occasionally come loose, another option is to have a licensed veterinarian implant a microchip under your dog's skin. It can store vital data including contact, license, and vaccination information, and many animal shelters often scan for these chips when dogs are found without ID. Numbered tattoos are another method and are common with some breeds like golden retrievers. The best solution, however, is to keep your dog on a leash or under voice control at all times.

Co-author Ashley Goodrich and Rebel on the Appalachian Trail near Woody Gap

Conditioning

Hiking and backpacking are often very different than walking with your pet in an urban park. Hiking is frequently much more strenuous and takes place over rugged terrain that in the South can vary from sandy marsh to rocky or root-laden soils. Dogs, like humans, get sore muscles, stiff legs, and bruised and blistered feet. If this is your first hike (or just your first trip with your canine), then start with the "Easy" hikes in this book and gradually work up to the "Difficult" ones. Mix in some urban jaunts during the week, and eventually your strength and stamina will increase to the point where even the "Difficult" trails are within reach for you and your pet.

Keep in mind that not all breeds are created equal, and some dogs will have an easier time than others adjusting to life on the trail. We have hiked with over fifteen breeds, and each responded differently to the experience. Smaller dogs (like the Jack Russell terrier and schnauzer) work much harder since they have smaller legs, and have more difficulty maneuvering across streams and rivers. Short-haired dogs (like the Lab) do better in the South's hot and humid summer weather, while long-haired dogs (like the golden retriever and husky) thrive in the colder winter months, particularly at higher elevations. Whatever the breed, all dogs excel to some degree in the wilderness. Their energy and excitement are apparent as soon as they get their first whiff of the smells of the trail.

The best advice is to test your dog on urban walks before you hit the wilderness. Know what he is capable of, and learn your pet's language for when he is tired, hungry, thirsty, and agitated. Test his tolerance of other animals before your reach the trailhead, and get some dog obedience training in your hometown.

The Essentials
Gear for You

The first question we are often asked is where to hike in Georgia and South Carolina. The second is what to take on the trail. As with any sport, the right gear can make a major difference in how much you enjoy the wilderness experience. For starters, every hiker should have the Ten Essentials, which were first described in the 1930s by The Mountaineers.

The Ten Essentials: A Systems Approach

1. **Navigation (map and compass or GPS).** A map and compass are critical to your travel in the wilderness. They should have enough detail and dimension (topography, trails, roads, campsites, towns, etc.) to help you navigate on the trail, and you also need the skills and knowledge to use them correctly. If you are unfamiliar with their use, take a class at a local outfitter or community college (the latter may offer courses via ROTC classes). You might also consider joining an orienteering club. For some hikers, a GPS may be an easier alternative, especially if it comes equipped with topographical maps. Whatever the case, take some form of navigational tool into the wilderness. It will be indispensable in areas that lack trail signs or blazes.

2. **Sun protection (sunglasses and sunscreen).** We are blessed with lots of sunshine in the South, so sunglasses and sunscreen are very important year round, especially when the trees are barren and hikers are exposed to the winter sun. Surprisingly, sunscreen is more of a necessity in the winter than in the summer, when the thick foliage prevents the sun's rays from beating down on the trail.

3. **Insulation (extra clothing).** Extra clothing protects a hiker from shrubs, thorns, insects, sun, wind, and cold. Multiple layers are generally warmer and more versatile than a single garment, and when kept dry they help prevent hypothermia. Always keep a set of dry, insulating clothing on hand and stored in a waterproof container (we usually line a stuff sack with a garbage bag). In an emergency, clothing has many uses and can be cut into bandages, made into a pillow, used as a hot pad, towel, or climbing line.

4. **Illumination (headlamp or flashlight).** Traveling in the dark is dangerous, and a flashlight will help protect you against physical injury. It will also help you find your way, identify things in your pack, observe wildlife, or signal for assistance during a backcountry emergency. To be safe, always carry extra bulbs and batteries.

5. **First-aid supplies.** A first-aid kit usually contains items to treat cuts, abrasions, blisters, punctures, and burns. Other items in the kit might fix broken bones, aid injured limbs, assist with cardiac conditions, or with frostbite, hypothermia, hypoxia, decompression

Glenn Schuffenhauer and Indy in a shelter on the Appalachian Trail during a cold October night

sickness, insect bites, allergic reactions, animal attacks, and thermal or chemical burns.

6. **Fire (firestarter and matches/lighter).** Matches and a firestarter are needed to light a stove or campfire, and may allow you to signal for aid or prevent hypothermia in an emergency situation.

7. **Repair kit and multi-tool (or knife).** A knife is helpful for eating, opening packages, building shelter, repairing gear, or even cutting rope cord. We also carry a small repair kit with a needle, thread, cement, and patch for the sleeping pad, and a mini tube of oil for the stove pump.

8. **Nutrition (extra food).** The mind is your most valuable asset in the wilderness. For it to work effectively, you need plenty of food. Prepare accordingly.

9. **Hydration (extra water).** Staying properly hydrated is critical in the backcountry. Always carry plenty of water, and make a mental note of any water sources that you pass on the trail in case you run out.

10. **Emergency shelter.** Even day hikers should carry a tarp or emergency space blanket. This could save your life and will help prevent hypothermia, one of the biggest dangers in the backcountry.

Many day hikers may question the need to take all of these items on a leisurely two-hour hike. However, it is important to "be prepared" (as the Boy Scout motto suggests). Every year, numerous visitors to our state and national forests get lost, find themselves ill-prepared, and end up spending an unplanned night in the wilderness. These items will ensure that, should this occur, your wilderness visit does not become a survival situation. The Mountaineers textbook *Mountaineering: The Freedom of the Hills* also recommends supplementing these Ten Essentials with the following:

- Water treatment device (filter or chemicals) and water bottles
- Insect repellent (or clothing designed for this purpose)
- Signaling devices, such as a whistle, cell phone, two-way radio, or flares

In addition to the Ten Essentials, we always carry raingear and a fleece jacket in case the weather changes rapidly. Thunderstorms are common in Georgia and South Carolina in the summer months and can drop the temperature by as much as 40 degrees after a heavy rain.

Overnight backpackers will naturally have a much larger gear list which will include a tent, sleeping bag, and sleeping pad at a minimum. For a complete checklist, you can visit our website at *www.n2backpacking.com*.

Gear for Your Dog

In the backcountry, your pet will rely on you for survival. It is your responsibility to make sure that your dog has plenty of food, remains hydrated, and has adequate shelter if you plan to camp overnight. For example, in November a few years ago we hiked the Blood Mountain Wilderness in North Georgia. A cold front rolled through at dusk and the temperatures dropped to 10 degrees during the night. We had forgotten our Lab's sleeping pad, and his fleece blanket was not adequate in the plummeting temperatures. As a result, we spent the entire night wrapped around our pet with a sleeping bag draped over us. The lesson is that you must have proper gear for both you *and* your pooch. Here is a list of a dog's Ten Essentials:

The Ten Canine Essentials

1. **Obedience training.** Before you set foot on a trail, make sure your dog is trained and behaves well with other hikers, dogs, and backcountry wildlife.
2. **Doggy backpack.** This lets your dog carry his own gear, which is particularly helpful on overnight backpacking trips. We recommend that your pet carry no more than a fourth of his body weight in a fully loaded doggy pack.
3. **Basic first-aid kit.** See the "Hazards" section for details.
4. **Dog food and trail treats.** Carry more food than your dog normally consumes since both of you will be burning more calories than normal. Trail treats also provide quick energy and a pick-me-up for your pup during a strenuous day hike or backpacking trip.
5. **Water and water bowl.** You cannot count on water being available along the trail, especially in the late summer and early fall when springs and streams start to dry up. So pack enough water to meet all your dog's drinking needs.
6. **Leash and collar, or harness.** Because many parks (especially state and national parks) require them, you should take a leash, collar, or harness even if your dog is well trained to voice commands. This is common courtesy on the trail and helps to keep wilderness areas available to you and your pooch.
7. **Insect repellent.** Some animals and some people have strong negative reactions to DEET-based repellents. For this reason, we recommend the use of non-DEET-based repellents such as Frontline or

Backpackers and their dogs at Rabun Gap on the Bartram Trail in North Georgia

K9 Advantix. Restrict repellent applications to those places the dog is unable to lick (like the back of the neck and around the ears).

8. **ID tags and picture identification.** Your dog should always wear identification on his collar, and microchips are highly recommended for dogs that spend time in the backcountry. These tiny encoded devices are placed between a dog's shoulders or under his skin. Lost dogs can be identified when a hand scanner is used by staff at animal control, a veterinarian clinic, shelter, or animal hospital. Microchips and hand scanning devices are so prevalent that almost every major facility regularly checks unidentified dogs that arrive for their services. If your dog gets lost, you should also have pictures

of the animal with you. This speeds the recovery efforts and allows you to post flyers and handbills in the surrounding communities if necessary.

9. **Dog booties.** Some dogs hate booties with a passion, but they can be very useful in rocky or harsh trail conditions or on long-distance hikes to avoid damaging your dog's pads. So carry booties with you just in case, particularly if you are deep in the backcountry. They may save the day for both you and your pooch.

10. **Compact roll of plastic bags and trowel.** Picking up after your pet is critical to maintaining goodwill in the wilderness for hikers and their dogs. So either bag the waste and carry it out, or dig a six-inch hole with a trowel (small shovel) to bury it. Lightweight, inexpensive plastic trowels are available at most backpacking stores.

In addition to these Ten Essentials, on overnight backpacking trips we always take a collapsible food bowl, water bottle, sleeping pad, and Paktowl for our dog. Ruffwear (*www.ruffwear.com*) makes a lightweight collapsible bowl that has a waterproof liner so it can be used for either food or water. CoolPooch (*www.coolpooch.com*) makes a water bottle that is convenient for both owner and pet. We also recommend a Paktowl since it is handy if your dog is wet or muddy and about to climb into the tent.

On overnight winter hikes, a sleeping bag can be a lifesaver for short-haired dogs. Our Lab gets cold in temperatures below 50 degrees, so we cut and sewed an old sleeping bag in half and it works great in the winter months. For smaller dogs, consider a quarter-sized cut, but be aware that not all pets like being confined to a sleeping bag. You might do better to wrap them in a warm blanket. Regardless of the breed, make sure to take a sleeping pad in addition to a sleeping bag. The cold ground literally sucks the heat out of any mammal, and your dog will be significantly warmer and happier with some type of sleeping pad, whether it is a foam mattress, fleece mat, or $15 camper's Ridge Rest (*www.cascadedesign.com*), available in most backpacking stores.

On day hikes, we rarely use the doggy backpack. For overnight trips, however, our Lab almost always carries his own gear. There are at least five major manufacturers of dog backpacks that offer a variety of shapes, sizes, and styles. We offer more specific advice on choosing and loading a dog backpack under "Backpacking and Camping with Your Dog," but our general recommendations are that the total loaded pack weight be no more than one-fourth the dog's body weight, and that you watch carefully for any chafing since your dog cannot tell you about a poor fit. Load the pack at home, adjust the straps, and try it out before you hit the trail.

On the Trail
Traveling with Your Dog

Now that you and your pet are geared up for the trail, it's time for the fun part—the hiking. Unless you are extremely fortunate, the trailhead is probably at least thirty minutes away. So first, here are a few tips for getting to the trailhead safely.

Chances are that your dog has ridden in the car before this trip. If not (or if your canine has never traveled any significant distance), try to make your pet as comfortable as possible. We put our dog's bed in the back of our SUV and usually throw a bone, tennis ball, or some type of toy in with him. While your dog may enjoy sitting on your lap (especially

Rebel takes a well-deserved break on the spur trail to Browns Mountain along the Kings Mountain National Recreation Trail.

smaller dogs like the Jack Russell terrier), this is extremely dangerous and is highly discouraged. Hikers with flat-bed pickup trucks should also be very careful transporting their animals and should get some type of carrier or pen if they ride in the back of the truck. The goal is to arrive at the trailhead safely so that you can enjoy the day.

In hot weather, avoid leaving your dog in the vehicle for any length of time, and crack all the windows to allow fresh air to circulate if you briefly leave the car or truck. When it is 80 degrees outside, the temperature inside the vehicle can soar to 150 degrees—particularly in the South's humid summer months. Allow fresh air in the vehicle, and make sure your pooch gets plenty of water and stays hydrated. Bright yellow urine is a sign that your dog is not getting enough water.

When you reach the trailhead, your pet will likely spazz out—excited for what the day has in store. Leash your dog before she gets out of the vehicle, especially if the park requires it or if other people (or animals) are in the area.

Ten Canons of Canine Trail Etiquette

When you finally hit the trail, it is important to remember that not all hikers appreciate dogs as much as we do. Not everyone has a canine or grew up around one. So do not expect them to laugh or smile when your dog runs, jumps, or barks at them—whether as a playful gesture or not. We have compiled this short list of guidelines to help summarize this point.

1. **Use a leash.** Put your dog on a leash, not just where required but when you meet other hikers and dogs on the trail. Otherwise, make sure your dog is under voice control at all times and responds to it.

2. **Stay on the trail.** This helps prevent erosion, and makes it more difficult for your dog to get lost. Wild animal encounters are also less frequent when your dog is on the trail and not roaming the wilderness.

3. **Yield to other hikers.** If another hiker approaches, step to the side of the trail, keep your leashed dog close to you, and let the other hiker(s) pass.

4. **Yield to horses, mountain bikers.** Some of the hikes in this book share portions of trail with horses and mountain bikers. Hold your dog close during these encounters, stay still, and let the others pass. The situation is more dangerous for them since they can be knocked off their horse or bike by an aggressive or overly excited canine.

5. **Greet other outdoor adventurers.** This breeds goodwill and ensures that your dog sees the other outdoorsman as a friend and not a foe.

6. **No more than two dogs.** When on the trail, keep the number of dogs to no more than two in your group. Any more is a pack, which means the animals will be much harder to control.

7. **Clean up after your pet.** There is nothing worse than stepping on a steaming pile in the middle of the trail. At the bare minimum, make sure your dog does not take a dump on the trail. Clean up after your dog by digging a cathole and burying the waste six to eight inches deep. Another option is to simply pack out the waste in a tightly sealed plastic bag.

8. **Obey the rules.** Other than keeping you and your pooch out of

Michael Crook and Rebel playing tug-of-war before hitting the trail

trouble, this will also ensure that you do not ruin the experience for the rest of us.

9. **Leave wild animals alone.** As you will read in the "Hazards" section, wild animals can be a real problem for a dog. This is for their protection, trust us.

10. **Be courteous around the campsite.** This means no begging, barking, growling, etc. It also means respecting other hikers' rights to enjoy themselves without your dog raiding their food, stomping across their sleeping pad (or bag), or tracking muddy paws into their tent.

By following proper canine etiquette, you are ensuring that owners everywhere can enjoy the wilderness experience with their pet—which in many cases is an extended member of their family. Remember that hiking with your dog is not a right but a privilege that can easily be taken away by a management agency due to thoughtless or disrespectful owners.

Leave No Trace

While we are on the subject of trail etiquette, it is also worth publishing some guidelines commonly known as Leave No Trace practices for the wilderness. These generally accepted principles (which you will find on just about every park brochure, map, or guide) are pretty self-explanatory and similar in scope to proper dog etiquette:

1. Plan ahead and prepare
2. Travel and camp on durable surfaces
3. Dispose of waste properly
4. Leave what you find
5. Minimize campfire impacts
6. Respect wildlife
7. Be considerate of other visitors

Backpacking and Camping with Your Dog

We have covered most of the things you need to know about backpacking and camping earlier in this section, but let us reiterate that dogs should not carry more than one-fourth of their body weight on the trail. If they carry any gear, it should be their own equipment, and it should be evenly balanced across their shoulder blades. Watch for chafing, and remove the pack if your dog starts to fall behind the group, shows signs of fatigue, pain, or looks generally unhappy. Doggy packs should be waterproof, padded, and have some type of system to secure it against your pet's body without restricting movement.

We like the packs that have a separate harness and backpack. This makes it easier to remove the main pack during a break, or at a stream or river crossing. Never let your dog cross a stream or river with a full pack. Weighed down, your pet may drown, particularly in the waist-deep streams that are common in Georgia and South Carolina.

While camping with your dog, make sure he does not bother other people at your campsite (see "Ten Canons of Canine Trail Etiquette"). Although many backcountry sites in the national forests do not require that dogs be leashed, it is a good idea in the evening hours when wildlife begins to stir. The last thing you need is for your pooch to tangle with a skunk or porqupine 5 miles from the nearest vehicle—which brings us to the next section.

Hazards

We have hiked countless miles with our Lab, and we have found the backcountry to be no more dangerous than the average backyard in urban

Charlie Brady and Rebel just before sunset near Blood Mountain

America. Our most harrowing experience was in the Slickrock Creek Wilderness in North Carolina, when our dog was swept down a four-foot waterfall by a current that moved faster than he did. Fortunately, he survived the incident without injury and our hope is that these tips will also make your ventures into the wilderness trouble-free.

Weather

The single biggest hazard in the backcountry is weather. Hikers and backpackers should never underestimate Mother Nature and should always be prepared for rain, sleet, or even an occasional snow shower. Conditions can change rapidly in the mountains of Georgia and South Carolina, even during the summer months, and hypothermia (where the body cannot maintain its core temperature) is the biggest danger for a hiker and his/her dog. To prevent hypothermia in foul weather, stay dry if possible and seek shelter immediately. Drink hot fluids and eat food or snacks if they are available. Typically, a 40-degree rain on the trail is much more dangerous than a 20-degree snow.

Lightning is also a major killer in the backcountry. It tends to strike prominent objects and can occur at any time of year in Georgia and South Carolina. This book features some trails across open summits, so use extreme caution in the summer months if you notice a thunderstorm approaching. The best advice is to descend immediately and try to find the lowest ground possible. If that is not an option, most experts recommend that you sit on a backpack or foam pad and remain in a crouched position to minimize the ground currents from a nearby strike.

Many dogs are afraid of thunder and lightning and may freak out as the storm approaches. If you are pinned down, try to create a safe place for your pet using a tent, tarp, or rain jacket. You can also try to distract your dog with a tennis ball, treat, or small stick. The goal is to give your dog a sense of comfort and security, and to protect yourself in the process.

Heat and humidity are more of a nuisance than anything. Hikers and their dogs should stay properly hydrated, slow down their pace, and take breaks if they start to feel nauseated.

Snow in moderation (1 to 3 inches) is rarely much of a problem in the South. Hiking and routefinding are more difficult, but some hikers and long-haired breeds actually find it more enjoyable than backpacking in the heat and humidity. During the winter, avoid getting caught in a blizzard by carrying a small AM/FM radio or NOAA weather radio. For multi-day backpacking trips in the mountains of north Georgia and

Rebel finds a big stick floating in a North Georgia river.

northwestern South Carolina, this is highly recommended, especially in January and February.

Animals

It is far more likely that your dog will tangle with a small animal like a porcupine or skunk than a large animal like a wild boar or bear. Georgia and South Carolina have all of these wild critters, but it is unlikely that you will have an issue—especially if your dog is on a leash. Most wildlife is active in the morning and evening, so be particularly careful at these times.

Black bears are plentiful in Georgia and South Carolina and typically weigh between 200 and 500 pounds. The state wildlife agencies have a strictly controlled hunting season from September to December, so most bears fear people and usually are not a problem. To be sure, hang all your food while backcountry camping and avoid a bear encounter whenever possible. Bears (like humans) are unpredictable. Do not feed or approach or run from a bear, and only fight back as a last resort. For the record, the grizzly (or brown bear) does not live in the eastern United States, so there is no need to be concerned about them while hiking or camping in Georgia and South Carolina.

Wild pigs, also called feral hogs, have been in North America since 1539, when the first European settlers brought them to Florida as domestic pigs. Another race of wild pig, the European wild boar, was released in New Hampshire, North Carolina, Missouri, Arkansas, and Tennessee in the late 1800s and early 1900s for the purpose of hunting. You may see wild boar, particularly in the Congaree Swamp of South Carolina or the Cohutta Wilderness of Georgia. Although sightings are rare and wild boar are generally fearful of people, they can be very dangerous to a dog due to their long hard tusks. The best advice is to keep dogs leashed in these areas, or anywhere that wild boar are abundant.

The most likely encounter on the trail for your pet is with small game—the bobcat, fox, porcupine, or skunk. Although these species do not typically present a life-threatening situation for your pooch, most dogs will immediately give chase to these animals when given an opportunity, and this could result in an unpleasant response. Make sure your dog's rabies vaccination is up-to-date, and be aware that unleashed dogs may need a vet's attention if they tangle with one of these critters.

Alligators

South Georgia and coastal Carolina are heavily populated with alligators (but have no crocodiles). Although alligators rarely threaten or attack humans, small dogs are a common target. Use extra caution in the Low Country (especially in the Congaree and I'on Swamps), and stay on the trail to avoid any unwelcome encounters.

Snakes

Georgia and South Carolina have four species of poisonous snakes: the coral snake, copperhead, cottonmouth, and rattlesnake. Again, the best way to avoid them is to stay on the trail, particularly in rocky, swampy, or wet areas.

According to the U.S. Food and Drug Administration, about 8000 people a year receive venomous snakebites in the United States, and only nine to fifteen victims (0.2 percent) die. So, chances are good that either you or your pet will survive the bite since venom is only injected in roughly 50 percent of the bites.

Snakebite kits are generally shunned by the medical community and often do more harm than good. When bitten by a snake, a hiker should remain calm, get safely away from the snake, and watch the afflicted area. If it swells significantly or turns black, have someone call 911 (or the emergency number in your area) for help. Have the victim lie down and keep the affected limb immobilized and lower than the heart. Venom will spread more slowly through the body and cause less damage if movement is kept to a minimum.

Insects

Fleas, ticks, mosquitos, and stinging insects are a nuisance both at home and in the backcountry—particularly between late spring and early fall when the weather is warm in Georgia and South Carolina. Fleas feed on animal blood and can trigger problems including skin irritation, allergic reactions, anemia, and in rare cases, death. They can also carry tapeworms, which can infest your pet. If you see small rice-like particles around the dog's anus or in his feces, he probably has tapeworms and you should seek medical attention immediately.

Ticks can carry serious diseases such as Lyme, ehrlichiosis, babesiosis, and Rocky Mountain spotted fever. Three of the more common tick species found in the South are the lone star tick, the American dog tick (sometimes known as the wood tick), and the blacklegged tick (also known as the deer tick). In Georgia and South Carolina, the lone star tick is the most common of the species, and it resembles a pinhead in size. Adults are about ⅛-inch long and brown, and adult females have a white spot in the middle of their backs. The lone star tick is sometimes misidentified as the blacklegged or deer tick because they are so similar in size.

Although it can transmit Rocky Mountain spotted fever, the lone star tick is not as likely to transmit the disease as the American dog tick, which may also spread tularemia and ehrlichiosis to humans. The American dog tick is the second most common tick found in the South, and it feeds on humans and medium to large mammals such as raccoons and dogs. Unfed males and females are reddish-brown and about ³⁄₁₆-inch long. Females have a large silver-colored spot behind the head and will become ½-inch long after feeding. Males have fine silver lines on the back and do not get much larger after gorging themselves. Sometimes males are mistaken for other species of ticks because they appear so different than the female. The American dog tick can transmit Rocky Mountain spotted fever, tularemia, and possibly ehrlichiosis to humans, but must be attached for at least four hours to cause illness.

The blacklegged or deer tick will feed on a variety of hosts including both humans and wildlife (such as deer). The adult tick is reddish-brown and about ⅛-inch long, or about one-half the size of the more familiar female American dog tick. The blacklegged or deer tick is found in wooded areas along trails and can transmit Lyme disease and possibly ehrlichiosis to humans. However, the tick must be attached at least 24 hours to cause illness.

Rocky Mountain spotted fever is the most common disease caused by ticks in Georgia and South Carolina. The disease can appear as flu-like symptoms and cause a rash on the body, face, palms of the hands, and soles of the feet. It can be treated with medicine but if left untreated is occasionally deadly.

Lyme disease also appears as flu-like symptoms with swollen lymph nodes and a rash resembling a bulls-eye at the site of the bite. Symptoms include joint pain and swelling, a stiff neck, headache, and an irregular heart rhythm. This disease is not deadly but can cause major health problems for humans. Ehrlichiosis can also appear as flu-like symptoms, confusion, and a rash anywhere on the body. It, too, is not deadly but can cause major health problems, while tuleremia can appear as a slow-growing ulcer at the site of the bite and cause swollen lymph nodes.

To protect your dog from fleas, ticks, and mosquitos, use a topical product like Frontline or K9 Advantix and make sure the application stays up to date. Do not use DEET-based insect repellants on pets since some are extremely sensitive to the chemical and may develop neurological problems if a product formulated with DEET is applied to their skin. You should also regularly use a preventative medication for heartworm, since mosquitoes transmit spirochetes year-round in Georgia and South Carolina.

Hikers and backpackers, in contrast, should consider a DEET-based repellant like *Off* for protection from unwanted pests. Long pants are also advised, particularly in the summer months when ticks are the most active. Tuck the pant leg into your socks and your shirt under your waist line. Ticks normally move up toward the head in these conditions and it is much easier to find them under these circumstances. Check for ticks twice per day, and if you find one grip the head as close to the skin as possible. Steadily pull upward until the tick releases from the body and do not twist or jerk the tick since you might break off the head or mouth parts. Avoid leaving the tick head embedded in the skin and do not squeeze to the point of crushing the tick because disease-spreading secretions may be released. If you do not have tweezers or a tick scoop, you can use your fingers, a loop of thread around the jaws, or a needle between the jaws to pull it out. Because all three of the tick species in Georgia and South

Carolina are similar in size and appearance, it is best to remove them as soon as possible and monitor any symptoms that may occur.

Bees and wasps are another common insect in the wilderness, and they are also particularly active in the late summer. Yellow jackets, which often take residence in the ground, can be extremely annoying to hikers and their dogs. If you or your pet gets stung, remove the stinger immediately, check for an allergic response, and then treat the sting. Owners may benefit from a dose of Benadryl and dogs may appreciate a home remedy of baking soda, toothpaste, meat tenderizers or raw onion slices applied to the sting—although the verdict is out if it's truly effective. If you are allergic to bees or wasps, make sure to plan accordingly with an oral antihistamine (like Benadryl) or a prescription epinephrine injector pen. Although rare, bees and other insects kill more people annually than predators such as alligators, cougars, and bears—mainly due to allergic reactions.

Plants

There are three types of poisonous plants in Georgia and South Carolina: poison ivy, posion oak, poison sumac. Each contains a lacquer-like resin in their sap, urushiol, which has an active substance that irritates the skin. The old adage "Leaves of three, let it be" applies here since the distinguishing characteristics of these plants is a group of three leaflets.

Dogs do not usually get poison ivy, since their fur acts as a barrier from the resin. However, humans can transfer the resin to their skin by touching or coming into close contact with their pooch. Clothing or hiking gear may also transfer the urushiol and induce a reaction. Be aware that if you build a campfire, smoke from burning ivy plants may carry the resin and can affect all uncovered parts of the body. If the smoke from the plant is inhaled, it can also cause other problems.

The effects may not become apparent for a few hours, but eventually the skin reddens and begins to itch. Small, watery blisters may appear, and ultimately the itching will become more intense. The best treatment is calamine lotion or hydrocortisone or some type of oral steroid medication from a doctor. Healing usually takes two to four weeks.

Other Hazards

Hunting season is another hazard to consider, especially in the winter months. Most hunters are outdoor enthusiasts just like you and often have dogs themselves. However, as a precaution, both you and your pet should always wear bright orange clothing during hunting season.

Terrain can be another danger in the backcountry of Georgia and South Carolina. The mountains have many fast-moving waterfalls and streams which can put both owner and pet in a precarious situation. Watch for slippery conditions near steep cliffs and cascading waterfalls. Never cross a stream or river in fast-moving or rising water, and never let your dog attempt a crossing with a full pack. Always unbuckle the straps of your pack before traversing any body of water.

As a summary to this section, we have provided a doggy first-aid kit to to help you in the backcountry. Consider it one of your Ten Essentials, and you and your pet will be prepared for many miles in the wilderness.

First Aid for Your Dog

It is necessary to have a first-aid kit for your dog, even if it contains only the bare essentials. You never know when your pooch might decide to tangle with a porky (or porcupine, as they are more commonly known). For a complete, comprehensive canine kit, consider the following:

Instruments
Scissors/bandage scissors/toenail clippers
Rectal thermometer (a healthy dog should show a rectal
   temperature of 101 degrees)

Cleansers and disinfectants
Hydrogen peroxide, 3 percent
Betadine
Canine eyewash (available at any large pet-supply store)

Topical antibiotics and ointments (nonprescription)
Calamine lotion
Triple antibiotic ointment (Bacitracin, Neomycin, or Polymyxin)
Baking soda (for bee stings)
Vaseline
Stop-bleeding powder

Medications
Enteric-coated aspirin or Bufferin
Imodium-AD
Pepto-Bismol

Dressings and bandages
Gauze pads (4 inches square) or gauze roll
Nonstick pads
Adhesive tape (1- and 2-inch rolls)

Miscellaneous
Muzzle
Dog booties
Any prescription medication your dog needs

For extended trips, consult your vet about prescription medications that may be needed in emergency situations, including:
Oral antibiotics
Eye/ear medications
Emetics (to induce vomiting)
Pain medications and anti-inflammatories
Suturing materials for large open wounds

Using This Book
About the Hikes
The hikes in the guidebook are described with three modes of travel in mind:
1. In-and-out, backtrack hikes
2. Loop hikes
3. One-way, shuttle hikes

Since most people prefer loop hikes, the majority of routes featured in the book do not require you to backtrack or shuttle a car. Main trails are marked with dark lines, while side trails are lighter in color. Major campgrounds, backcountry campsites, and shelters are shown on each map, with trailheads and points of interest flagged and detailed. Trail conditions are rated from easy to difficult and vary significantly throughout the guidebook. Each hike may have some or all of the following characteristics:

1. **Easy.** The trails are short (less than 3 miles), easy to follow, well marked, and well maintained. The terrain is gentle on a dog's pads, has very little elevation change (under 500 feet), and has no regular hazards for the hiker and their canine companion. It is suitable for any dog of any size and age.
2. **Easy to Moderate.** As the name implies, the trail is somewhere between "Easy" and "Moderate."
3. **Moderate.** The trails are longer (4–8 miles), fairly easy to follow, occasionally marked and maintained, and meet the requirements of the average hiker. The terrain may have sections that are rocky,

rough, or tough on the feet, and likely has some rolling hills and elevation change (up to 1000 feet). There may also be an occasional hazard like a creek crossing or steep cliff. Under normal conditions, the trail is suitable for the average hiker and the average dog.

4. **Moderate to Difficult.** As the name implies, the trail is somewhere between "Moderate" and "Difficult."

5. **Difficult.** The trail is long, particularly for day hikers (8 or more miles), or the route can be difficult to follow, and is not well marked or maintained. There may be some very strenuous sections with a lot of elevation change (more than 1000 feet), and difficult creek crossings, steep and unprotected cliffs, or challenging backcountry conditions may exist. These hikes are suitable for only experienced hikers and fit, trail-hardened dogs.

Our goal in this guidebook is to offer some of the best hikes with dogs in Georgia and South Carolina. The "Hike Summary Table" gives an overview of a variety of attributes that you can review to find the trail that is right for you and your pet. We have tried to offer a variety of trail conditions so that there is a suitable hike regardless of your dog's breed and overall level of fitness. We sincerely hope this book lives up to your expectations and that it helps to get you out and off the couch to enjoy some of the scenic miles of city, state, and federal hiking trails in Georgia and South Carolina.

A Note About Safety

Safety is an important concern in all outdoor activities. No guidebook can alert you to every hazard or anticipate the limitations of every reader. Therefore, the descriptions of roads, trails, routes, and natural features in this book are not representations that a particular place or excursion will be safe for your party. When you follow any of the routes described in this book, you assume responsibility for your own safety. Under normal conditions, such excursions require the usual attention to traffic, road and trail conditions, weather, terrain, the capabilities of your party, and other factors. Keeping informed on current conditions and exercising common sense are the keys to a safe, enjoyable outing.

The Mountaineers Books

PART 2

Georgia

NORTHERN GEORGIA

1. Conasauga River

Round trip: 3.2 miles
Difficulty: Moderate to difficult
Hiking time: 2–3 hours
High point: 2297 feet
Elevation gain: 505 feet
Best season: Summer
Maps: Cohutta and Big Frog Wilderness; USGS Tennga Quad
Contact: Chattahoochee National Forest, Armuchee-Cohutta Ranger District, 3941 Highway 76, Chatsworth, GA 30705, (706) 695-6736, *www.fs.fed.us/conf*

Getting there: (From Atlanta, GA, 2 hours; from Chatsworth, GA, 40 minutes) At the intersection of Route 52 and US 411 in Chatsworth, follow US 411 north for 7.3 miles to Grassy Street. Turn right onto Grassy Street just after the Crandall post office, and continue on Grassy Street until you come to a set of railroad tracks. After crossing the tracks, turn right onto Crandall-Ellijay Road. Continue for 0.1 mile, and watch the road carefully. Turn left onto Forest Road 630 (also known as Mill Creek Road) and follow Forest Road 630 (which becomes gravel after 0.5 mile) for about 9 miles to a four-way intersection with Forest Road 17. Continue straight across Forest Road 17 to the parking area.

The Conasauga River is a favorite destination in north Georgia for both hikers and their dogs, and it is particularly worthy in the warm summer months when fishing and swimming are possible in the many shallow pools tucked along the scenic river. For overnight backpackers, there are

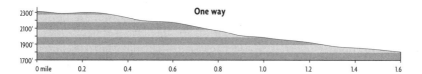

numerous campsites along the Conasauga, and this is a great wilderness experience for anyone who appreciates the remote and rustic woodlands that are characteristic of the national forests. The Conasauga River drainage is very popular with all types of outdoorsmen, including hikers, hunters, fishermen, and horsemen, so don't expect complete solitude without hiking deep into the Cohutta Wilderness.

The hike to the Conasauga River is an in-and-out hike following the Hickory Creek Trail from the parking area at Forest Road 630. The trail is not marked in the wilderness area (with the exception of pale green blazes at the river crossings). Nonetheless, the route is easily followed to the river on a wide path that was once a route for trains that harvested timber out of the Conasauga drainage in the early 1900s. The path makes a gradual, well-graded descent through a series of hardwoods and is a pleasant walk at any time of year.

As the trail levels and crosses Rough Creek to the Conasauga, the Hickory Creek Trail comes to an abrupt halt and meets the Conasauga

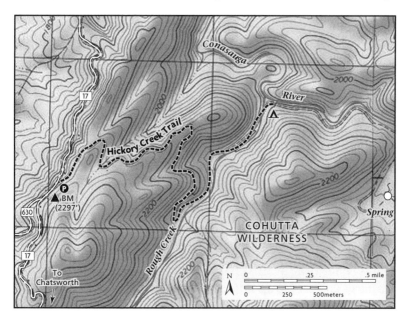

Major gnaws on a stick after a long day swimming in the Conasauga River.

River Trail at the water. Here the hike either continues on the Conasauga River Trail across the river (which requires wading in water that is occasionally knee-deep), or it turns right on the combined Conasauga River and Hickory Creek Trails and follows the river.

For those interested in a leisurely day hike, this is a great place to stop and take a break along the banks of the Conasauga before the long ascent back to the parking area at Forest Road 630. The river offers an excellent opportunity to swim or fish, and your dog will likely enjoy the river as much as you do. Overnight backpackers will find many campsites in this area and along the Conasauga River Trail, but please pack out any trash found here since it is heavily used and occasionally abused.

The Forest Service wanted a note in this guidebook regarding the nearby (and extremely popular) Jacks River Falls area. Due to overuse, the wilderness has been closed as of June 2006 to overnight campers, and fires are no longer permitted at any time of the year. This will allow the Jacks River Falls area time to revegetate and recover from years of heavy use.

2. Toccoa River

Round trip: 7 miles
Difficulty: Moderate to difficult
Hiking time: 4.5 hours
High point: 2726 feet
Elevation gain: 875 feet
Best season: Summer, fall
Map: USGS Wilscot Quad
Contact: Chattahoochee National Forest, Toccoa Ranger District, 6050 Appalachian Highway, Blue Ridge, GA 30513, (706) 632-3031, *www.fs.fed.us/conf*

Getting there: (From Atlanta, GA, 1.75 hours; from Dahlonega, GA, 1 hour) In Dahlonega, take US 19 and Route 60 north for 9 miles. Bear left on Route 60, where US 19 turns right. Then continue another 7 miles to Suches. From the intersection of Routes 180 and 60 in Suches, continue north on Route 60 for another 14.8 miles to the Route 60 trailhead. Roadside parking is along the right side of the road, just beyond the trail crossing.

The Benton MacKaye Trail and the Duncan Ridge Trail share this in-and-out route between Route 60 and the Toccoa River, and the highlight of this section is an impressive suspension bridge over the river. The Georgia Appalachian Trail Conference and the U.S. Forest Service constructed the 260-foot bridge in 1977, and it offers an excellent view of the Toccoa River in both directions.

The trail begins near Tooni Gap, located on Route 60 at 2028 feet, and heads south over Tooni Mountain toward the river. In the first mile, the Benton MacKaye and Duncan Ridge Trails make an ascent of nearly 600 feet up Tooni Mountain (sometimes referred to as Toonowee Mountain

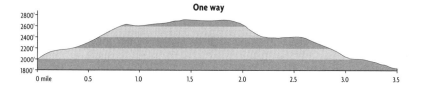

Robbie Gomez and Rebel cross the suspension bridge over the Toccoa River.

on older maps). Tooni Mountain is actually a series of small knobs across a long ridgeline with elevations that range from 2396 to 2720 feet. The result is a bouncy ride for hikers and their dogs as they traverse these knobs before the Benton MacKaye and Duncan Ridge Trails make their final descent after 3.5 miles to the Toccoa River at 1920 feet.

At the river, the trail flattens out and turns to the right toward the Toccoa River suspension bridge. This area is particularly appealing in the summer months, with opportunities to swim, fish, or paddle in the water. The rapids are rarely more than Class I, so both hikers and their dogs can

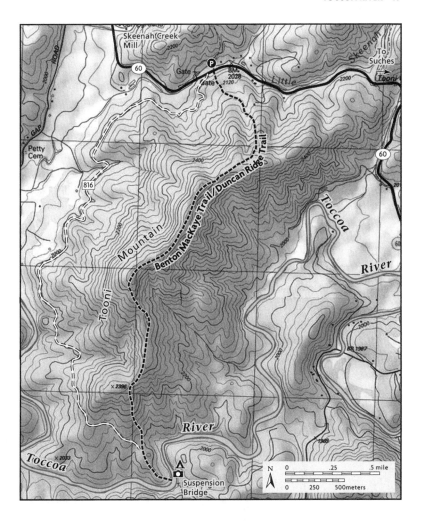

usually swim if the mood strikes. Forest Road 816 ends a short 0.3 mile from the suspension bridge, so don't expect a lot of privacy—even in the winter months. On the return hike, however, the gravel Forest Road 816 can be used to save some time and effort since it has very little elevation change as it winds back to Tooni Gap.

Overnight backpackers should opt for one of the numerous campsites across the river, but please pack out any trash found in this area since it is heavily used and occasionally abused. A four-wheel-drive vehicle is recommended on Forest Road 816 since the gravel road is bumpy and occasionally rutted closer to the river.

3. Green Mountain

Round trip: 1.9 miles
Difficulty: Moderate
Hiking time: 1–1.5 hours
High point: 2524 feet
Elevation gain: 370 feet
Best season: Early spring, late fall, winter
Map: USGS Blue Ridge Quad
Contact: Chattahoochee National Forest, Toccoa Ranger District,
6050 Appalachian Highway, Blue Ridge, GA 30513,
706 632-3031, *www.fs.fed.us/conf*

Getting there: (From Atlanta, GA, 2.5 hours; from Ellijay, GA, 15 minutes) At the junction of Route 5 and US 76 in Blue Ridge, take US 76 east 0.7 mile to Windy Ridge Road and turn right; drive for a short distance. At the three-way stop, turn left and continue 0.1 mile. Just ahead, turn right onto Aska Road. Continue 4.5 miles to the Deep Gap parking area where there is a small gravel lot on the right.

A summit sign marking the heavily forested Green Mountain

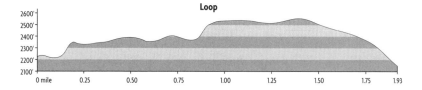

The Green Mountain Trail actually offers several hike options, including a loop from Deep Gap, a shuttle hike to Blue Ridge Lake, and a shuttle hike connecting with the Long Branch Loop Trail. This route, however, describes a loop hike from Deep Gap at Aska Road.

The white-blazed Green Mountain Trail begins across from the Deep Gap parking area on the other side of Aska Road. Going counterclockwise, start at the trailhead to the right with your back to the parking area. (The trailhead to the left, which is about 50 yards up Aska Road, is where the hike ends in about an hour.) The Green Mountain Trail gradually ascends on the southeastern side of Green Mountain on a well-marked dirt path through a canopy of hardwoods. There are excellent views of the surrounding mountains in this area (but only during the winter months).

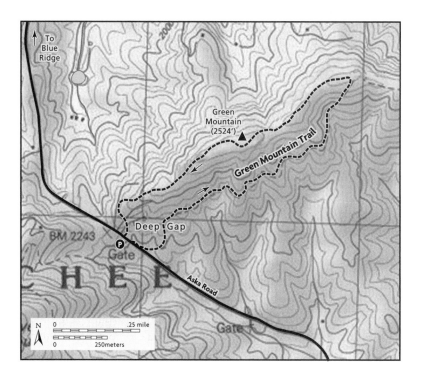

Just before the halfway point, the trail begins a steep ascent onto the ridge of Green Mountain. At the ridge crest, there is a wood sign and a junction with a trail leading 2.5 miles to Forest Road 711. Here the hike turns left and heads back toward Deep Gap for roughly a mile. (Going straight at the ridge crest will take you down to Blue Ridge Lake, which requires a car shuttle.) To complete the loop, turn left to begin a gradual ascent past the summit of Green Mountain. Once you see the wood sign marking the forested summit, the trail starts to drop in elevation, descending back to Aska Road about 50 yards from where you started.

The parking area at Aska Road is very busy, particularly on weekends, but this loop hike is short, well marked, and fairly user-friendly. Be careful when crossing Aska Road, especially with your pet, since vehicles occasionally come over the hill without warning.

4. Ramrock Mountain

Round trip: 2.8 miles
Difficulty: Easy to moderate
Hiking time: 1.5 hours
High point: 3200 feet
Elevation gain: 150 feet
Best season: Any season
Map: USGS Suches Quad
Contact: Chattahoochee National Forest, Brasstown Ranger
   District, 1881 Highway 515, P.O. Box 9, Blairsville, GA 30514,
   (706) 745-6928, *www.fs.fed.us/conf*

Getting there: (From Atlanta, GA, 1.5 hours; from Dahlonega, GA, 45 minutes) In Suches, take Route 60 1.6 miles south to Woody Gap. There are parking areas on both sides of the road and a large Forest Service sign that marks the gap. Park in the eastern parking area for access to Ramrock Mountain.

The walk to Ramrock Mountain is an in-and-out hike ideal for day-trippers, but it can also be done as an easy overnight backpacking trip. The hike begins on Route 60 at Woody Gap and follows the white blazes of the Appalachian Trail all the way to the rock outcropping that marks Ramrock Mountain (3200 feet).

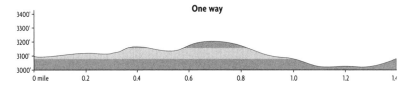

From the parking lot, the trail leads through a picnic area and begins a very gradual 1.4-mile ascent through a forest of hardwoods. The Appalachian Trail traverses the southern side of Black Mountain in the first mile, then descends slightly to Tritt Gap at 3050 feet. From here, the Appalachian Trail climbs nearly 200 feet over the next 0.4 mile to Ramrock Mountain, on the left. The rock outcropping has outstanding views to the south, and on a clear day turkey vultures are typically seen

Enjoying the views from Ramrock Mountain on a sunny spring day

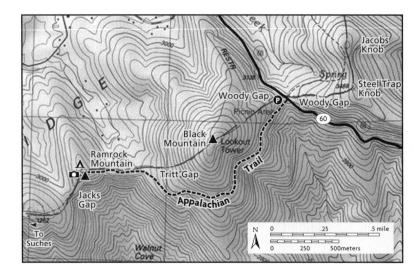

gliding through the skies (which may excite the pooch). From the vista, the start of the Appalachian Trail is roughly 20 trail miles to the west at Springer Mountain (see Hike 9).

For backpackers looking to make this an overnight adventure, there is a campsite to the northwest just across the trail from Ramrock Mountain. The National Forest Service does not currently require a backcountry permit to camp here, and there is enough room for a few tents.

5. Coosa Bald

Round trip: 12.8 miles
Difficulty: Difficult to very difficult
Hiking time: 6–8 hours
High point: 4270 feet
Elevation gain: 2150 feet
Best season: Any season
Maps: Chattahoochee National Forest, Blood Mountain Wilderness; USGS Neels Gap Quad
Fees and permits: Backpacing permit required for overnight camping. Fee is nominal.
Contact: Vogel State Park, 7485 Vogel State Park Road, Blairsville, GA 30512, (706) 745-2628, *www.gastateparks.org/info/vogel*

Getting there: (From Atlanta, GA, 2.5 hours; from Dahlonega, GA, 40 minutes) In Dahlonega, take US 19 north to Turners Corner, where US US 19 joins US 129. From here, continue north 10.5 miles to the Vogel State Park sign and entrance road. Rangers recommend you park at the visitor center due to limited trailhead parking. You can pick up a map here before hitting the trail.

For a nice, pleasant day hike with the dog, the Bear Hair Gap Trail (see Hike 6) is a gentle 4-mile loop in Vogel State Park. For a strenuous day hike or a challenging overnight backpacking trip, consider the Coosa Backcountry Trail. Located mostly within the boundaries of Vogel State Park, the route is a long and sometimes taxing hike that can take 6–8 hours to complete. For overnight camping, expect an 18–24-hour trip that requires a backcountry permit. The ranger station has up-to-date trail information on backcountry conditions and issues all-day and overnight trail permits; current restrictions and backcountry fees are listed on the Georgia state parks website, *www.gastateparks.org.*

The Coosa Backcountry Trail is best when hiked in a counterclockwise direction, since it offers a more gradual ascent to Coosa Bald. (The clockwise route makes a very aggressive ascent and it can also be more crowded, especially in the summer months due to some scenic waterfalls located near the junction with the Bear Hair Trail.) To begin this loop, follow the signs to the trail and turn right onto an old road at the 0.3-mile mark.

In the first 0.9 mile, the trail makes a gradual climb across Route 180 and continues on to Burnett Gap. Here the Coosa Backcountry Trail follows an old logging road and gradually descends to the West Fork of Wolf Creek where it crosses over a footbridge near Forest Road 107. After you walk across the dirt road, the trail begins a steep ascent through some hardwoods and eventually reaches Locust Stake Gap after 4.5 miles. Here you will find the first of several campsites.

From Locust Stake Gap, the trail continues on to Calf Stomp Gap about halfway through the loop at 6.6 miles. There is a small campsite

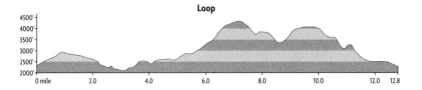

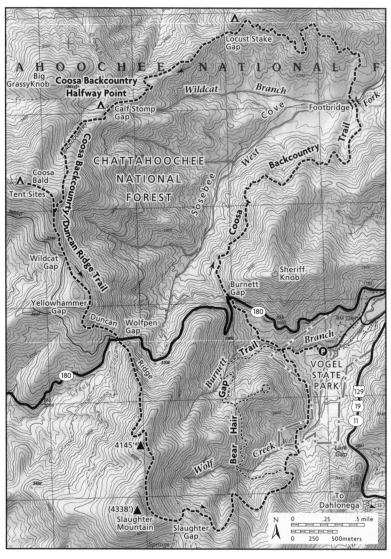

here along Forest Road 108 and water is nearby, located to the right and below the trail. Keep in mind that vehicles have access to this area and may occasionally travel through during the night. For those who decide to continue on to camp at Coosa Bald, now is a good time to fill up any water bottles and to make sure your dog enjoys a cool drink. The summit (which has some of the best campsites on the route) is dry, and this is your last chance to get water before you reach the Bald.

Hiking above the clouds on the Backcountry Trail with winter views from Coosa Bald to the east

This next section of the Coosa Backcountry Trail is very beautiful, especially in the spring and summer. It has winter views from a meadow that is sometimes covered with native spring wildflowers. A small portion of the trail traverses the Botanical Natural Area, and leaf collection baskets can occasionally be found here that are used to collect samples for wilderness nature studies.

From Calf Stomp Gap, the trail climbs gradually toward Coosa Bald and eventually intersects with the blue-blazed Duncan Ridge Trail near the summit. Follow it a short distance to reach the top of Coosa Bald at 4270 feet, the highest point on this hike. The best campsites on the trail are located on the summit, and there are also a few scattered tent sites along the trail. Coosa Bald has some fantastic winter views of the surrounding mountains, but don't expect to see much during the summer months. The wilderness has taken back most of what was once a wide, open meadow.

At the summit, the Coosa Backcountry Trail and the Duncan Ridge Trail combine and share the route back to the Vogel State Park. The trails reach the top of Wildcat Knob and eventually descend to Wolf-pen Gap where they cross Route 180 after 8.3 miles. The paved road is a good place to rest, because the next 0.5 mile is the steepest climb on the entire trail.

Route 180 gets a fair amount of traffic, so put your dog on a leash here or watch him very carefully. At the upper slopes of Slaughter Mountain at the 9.9-mile mark, the trail evens out and turns left to make a steep descent and joins with the Bear Hair Gap Trail, marked with orange blazes. The hike then follows the orange and yellow blazes the rest of the way back to the trailhead and the ranger station.

6. Bear Hair Gap Trail

Round trip: 3.5 miles
Difficulty: Moderate
Hiking time: 2 hours
High point: 3160 feet
Elevation gain: 800 feet
Best season: Any season
Map: USGS Coosa Bald Quad
Contact: Vogel State Park, 7485 Vogel State Park Road, Blairsville, GA
　　30512, (706) 745-2628, *www.gastateparks.org/info/vogel*

Getting there: (From Atlanta, GA, 2.5 hours; from Dahlonega, GA, 45 minutes) In Dahlonega, take US 19 north to Turners Corner, where US 19 joins US 129. From here, continue north 10.5 miles to the Vogel State Park sign and entrance road. Rangers recommend you park at the visitor center due to limited trailhead parking.

Vogel State Park, located at the base of Blood Mountain in the Chatta-hoochee National Forest, is one of Georgia's oldest and most popular facili-ties. The Bear Hair Gap Trail is the easier of the two routes in Vogel State

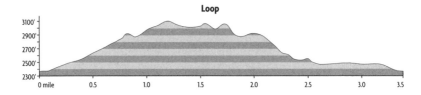

Park featured in this book (see also Coosa Bald, Hike 5), and is best suited for a day-hiker or anyone out for a leisurely afternoon with their dog.

The Bear Hair Gap Trail begins and ends in Vogel State Park. Because it is a loop hike, the trail can be hiked in either direction. However, most hikers prefer traveling the Bear Hair Gap Trail counterclockwise.

Begin at the trailhead in the southwestern corner of the park, just past some small rental cabins. Following the trail's orange blazes, walk along Burnett Branch (a water source), then turn south and wind along a side trail marked with green blazes after a little over a mile. This side trail leads to an overlook at 3160 feet with fantastic views of Lake Trahlyta to the northeast. Brasstown Bald, Georgia's highest peak, may also be seen in the distance northeast if the weather conditions are decent.

After a break at the overlook, follow the green blazes back to the orange-blazed Bear Hair Gap Trail and continue for another 2 miles back to Vogel State Park. On the way, the trail passes over an old dirt road and through a series of hardwoods. Then it intersects with the yellow-blazed

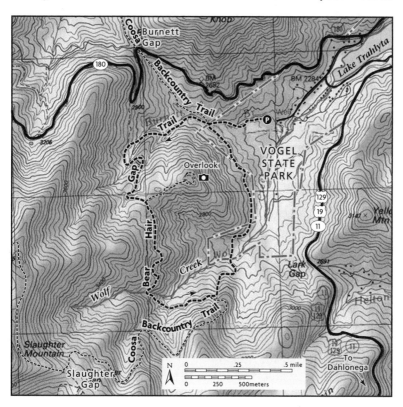

Steve Snyder departs the trailhead for some winter hiking along the Bear Hair Gap Trail.

Coosa Backcountry Trail, which shares the last few miles of this hike with the Bear Hair Gap Trail.

The area along Wolf Creek (another water source) is particularly interesting, as the stream cuts through a field of large boulders and winds its way through a series of large trees. As the trail turns northwest, leave Wolf Creek and return to Burnett Branch, near the start of the hike. The route turns right at this stream and retraces the first few steps back to the trailhead.

For those choosing to make this an overnight backcountry adventure, consider the Coosa Backcountry Trail (Hike 5), which requires a camping permit. Otherwise, Vogel State Park offers a variety of less rustic choices, including cottages and campsites near Lake Trahlyta. The park has 103 tent, trailer, and RV campsites, eighteen walk-in campsites, thirty-five cottages, four picnic shelters, a group shelter, and the pioneer campground. Pets are not allowed in or around cabins, so this may pose a problem for those who desire creature comforts and are planning an overnight stay with a dog. Pets are welcome, however, in the campgrounds if kept on a six-foot leash and attended at all times.

7. Blood Mountain

Round trip: 7.2 miles
Difficulty: Moderate to difficult
Hiking time: 3.5 hours
High point: 4461 feet
Elevation gain: 1461 feet
Best season: Spring or fall
Map: USGS Neels Gap Quad
Contact: Chattahoochee National Forest, Brasstown Ranger
   District, P.O. Box 9, Blairsville, GA 30512, (706) 745-6928,
   www.fs.fed.us/conf

Getting there: (From Atlanta, GA, 2.5 hours; from Dahlonega, GA, 45 minutes) In Dahlonega, take US 19/129 north for 22 miles to Neels Gap. Here the Appalachian Trail crosses the two-lane road, and the Walasi-Yi Center (a well-stocked backpacking store and hostel) is on the right with a parking area reserved for the store. Continue past Neels Gap and down the hill for 0.5 mile to a day and overnight parking lot for the Appalachian Trail. Take the second left off US 19/129 into the Reece State Memorial parking area.

Blood Mountain at 4461 feet is the highest point on the Appalachian Trail in the state of Georgia, and is a very popular destination for both overnight and day hikers since there are magnificent views from a rock outcropping at the summit. Blood Mountain and nearby Slaughter Gap were once the site of a major battle between the Cherokee and the Creek Indians. The summit is also known for an old stone shelter built by the Civilian Conservation Corps during the 1930s. It is listed in the National Register of Historic Places and is still used by hikers as a backcountry shelter.

As this loop hike begins, it leaves the Reece State Memorial parking

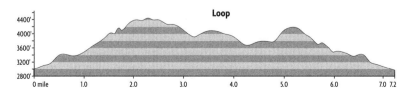

Charlie Brady and Rob Schwartz descend Blood Mountain via the Appalachian Trail on a crisp and sunny November morning.

area and ascends gradually along the blue-blazed Reece Memorial Trail. After 1 mile, it reaches the white-blazed Appalachian Trail (AT) at Flatrock Gap, where the loop turns right at a ridge to climb toward Blood Mountain. (Turning left on the Appalachian Trail leads down to Neels Gap, and going straight on the blue-blazed Freeman Trail leads down to Bird Gap.) Watch the route carefully at Flatrock Gap, and make sure to turn right and begin the ascent of Blood Mountain.

The trail to the summit is steep and is the most difficult section of this hike, with numerous switchbacks as you climb to the shelter. During the ascent, there are a few areas near the summit to take a break and enjoy the views. Both you and your dog will appreciate a lengthy rest at the top. It is recommended, however, to use a leash here since there are often a lot of hikers at Blood Mountain, particularly on weekends. The trail also borders a wildlife management area, and it is illegal to hike with an unleashed dog.

While on the summit, don't forget to check out the shelter register. The stone Blood Mountain Shelter sits on the 2175-mile Appalachian Trail at the 2.5-mile mark, and many thru-hikers stay here on their way from Georgia to Maine, often chronicling their journey in this and other

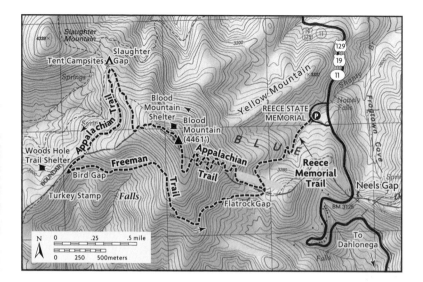

trail logs. Overnight backpackers can use the enclosed Blood Mountain Shelter, which can accommodate six to eight people on a first-come, first-served basis.

To descend Blood Mountain, continue northeast and follow the white blazes of the Appalachian Trail down toward Slaughter Gap at 3800 feet. The descent is a fairly easy hike with some more switchbacks and wonderful views to the north just beyond the summit. Hikers should watch the trail carefully when entering Slaughter Gap, since the blue-blazed Duncan Ridge Trail intersects with the Appalachian Trail here and leads to Route 180 at Wolfpen Gap.

A flat area just north of Slaughter Gap is an excellent backcountry campsite, with a seasonal spring located about 200 feet from the trail. The Forest Service prohibits campfires here and all along the Appalachian Trail from Slaughter Creek to Neels Gap (which includes Blood Mountain shelter area). Please respect the Forest Service regulations, and help this area recover from heavy use and occasional abuse.

From Slaughter Gap and the 3.4-mile mark, continue following the Appalachian Trail as it turns southwest and crosses two streams, descending gradually to Bird Gap at 3650 feet. The Woods Hole Shelter is located 0.4 mile off the AT, and the blue-blazed side trail is only 0.1 mile southwest from Bird Gap. Campfires are permitted in this location, and the shelter can accommodate twelve people with water available from a nearby spring.

To complete the loop, turn left on the blue-blazed Freeman Trail which intersects the Appalachian Trail after 4.4 miles at Bird Gap. The Freeman Trail gradually climbs back to Flatrock Gap at the 6.2-mile mark, then crosses the Appalachian Trail again and descends along the blue-blazed Reece Memorial Trail back to the parking area where the loop began at Route 19.

8. Frosty Mountain

Round trip: 11.8 miles
Difficulty: Moderate to difficult
Hiking time: 6–8 hours
High point: 3382 feet
Elevation gain: 1633 feet
Best season: Fall
Map: USGS Nimblewill Quad
Contact: Amicalola Falls State Park, 418 Amicalola Falls State Park Road Dawsonville, GA 30534, (706) 265-4703, *www.gastateparks.org/info/amicalola/*

Getting there: (From Atlanta, GA, 1 hour; from Dawsonville, GA, 15 minutes) At the intersection of Route 400 north, US 19 north, and Route 53 in Dawsonville (at the North Georgia Premium Outlet Mall), take Route 53 west for 9.3 miles. Veer right onto Route 183 and continue northbound for 10.8 miles to Route 52. At the junction of Routes 183 and 52, follow Route 52 approximately 3 miles to Amicalola Falls State Park, which is on the left. Trail maps are available at the visitor center.

Frosty Mountain is located in the Chattahoochee National Forest, a short distance from Amicalola Falls State Park. To hike this loop in a counterclockwise direction, start at the Amicalola Falls visitor center and follow the blue-blazed Approach Trail for 1.1 miles to the top of Amicalola Falls

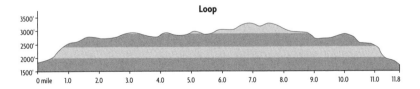

Susan Schuffenhauer rests at her campsite on Frosty Mountain with her dog, Indy.

near Amicalola Lodge. (There is a parking area here that eliminates the 700-foot ascent if you wish to shorten this hike and make it easier.) From the lodge, the Approach Trail crosses the road at the 1.2-mile mark and enters the woods. After a short distance, it meets a yellow-blazed side trail at the 1.4-mile mark, on the right, which leads to the Len Foote Hike Inn. Begin a gradual ascent, winding northeast through a forest of hardwood trees.

After 5 miles on the yellow-blazed trail, the Len Foote Hike Inn appears on a ridge near 3100 feet at 6.4 miles from the start at the visitor center. Named after Len Foote, who worked for thirty years as the southeastern field representative for the Wildlife Management Institute and eighteen years on the Georgia Game and Fish Commission and the Board of Natural Resources, the Hike Inn is designed for backcountry hikers who enjoy the wilderness but prefer some luxuries (including a comfy bed, warm showers, and hot food) over rustic backcountry camping. It was completed in the late 1990s and is accessible only by foot (except for the staff who drive in on an old Forest Road).

There are views at the Hike Inn to the east from the Star Base (a celestial calendar), which is on the opposite end of the property near the library. Pets are not allowed in any of the buildings or on the decks of the Len Foote Hike Inn, and are not permitted overnight. Please respect the rules set by Appalachian Education and Recreation Services (affiliated with the Georgia Appalachian Trail Club) and the Georgia Department of Natural Resources who manage this beautiful facility, and keep your dog on a leash at all times.

The trail continues past the Len Foote Hike Inn for another mile and eventually reaches the Approach Trail again at the 7.4-mile mark just

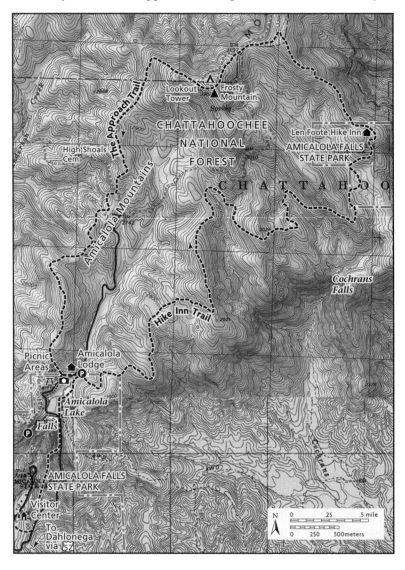

north of Frosty Mountain (3382 feet). Turn left at this trail junction, and follow the blue blazes heading southbound back to Amicalola Falls State Park. After 0.3 mile (and 7.7 miles from the start), the Approach Trail crosses Frosty Mountain Road (Forest Road 46), then makes a gradual ascent to Frosty Mountain at 8.0 miles.

The Frosty Mountain fire tower has been removed, but there is a seasonal spring and some flat areas for camping nearby. Backpackers who wish to make this an overnight adventure can camp at Frosty Mountain with their dog, or they can continue on to the Amicalola Falls State Park campground, which has twenty-four sites. (Pets are not allowed in or around the lodge.)

To finish the loop hike, leave Frosty Mountain, heading northwest. Then, at 9.6 miles, make a sharp turn to the southwest across High Shoals Road. The yellow-blazed Len Foote Hike Inn side trail will come into view again at the 10.4-mile mark, as will the Amicalola Lodge Road at 10.6 miles.

This loop hike finishes where it starts at the Amicalola Falls State Park visitor center, at 11.8 miles. It is a pleasant way to spend the day with your dog, whether you choose to make it a day or overnight hike.

9. Springer Mountain

Round trip: 4.5 miles
Difficulty: Moderate
Hiking time: 3.5 hours
High point: 3782 feet
Elevation gain: 680 feet
Best season: Any season
Map: USGS Noontootla Quad
Contact: Chattahoochee National Forest, 508 Oak Street NW, Gainesville, GA 30501, (706) 745-6928

Getting there: (From Atlanta, GA, 2 hours; from Blue Ridge, GA, 45 minutes) At the intersection of Route 400 north, US 19 north, and Route 53 in Dawsonville at the North Georgia Premium Outlet Mall, take Route 53 west for 9.3 miles to Route 183. Veer right at Route 183 and continue northbound for 10.8 miles to Route 52. Stay left at Route 52 and follow it northwest for 12 miles to Roy Road. Turn right onto Roy Road (the

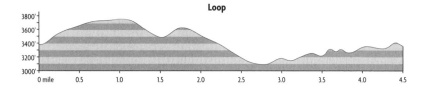

Loop

site of an old gas station) and continue 9.8 miles to a stop sign at the intersection of Nimbelwell Road. Turn right onto Nimbelwell Road, and drive 2.2 miles to a white church (Mount Pleasant Church) on the left and Forest Road 42 on the right. Turn right onto Forest Road 42 and follow a gravel road uphill for 6.8 miles to the Forest Road 42 parking area on the Appalachian Trail (AT). The start of the AT at Springer Mountain is a short 0.9-mile walk south on the Appalachian Trail from the parking area.

The summit of Springer Mountain marks the southern terminus of the Appalachian Trail, a 2172-mile long-distance trail that runs continuously from north Georgia to Mount Katahdin in northern Maine. Each spring, approximately 2500 hikers begin their long trek northbound from Springer Mountain, with plans to arrive in Maine by either September or October before the long, cold New England winter. Roughly 10 percent of thru-hikers travel north-to-south, however, and they typically complete their journey

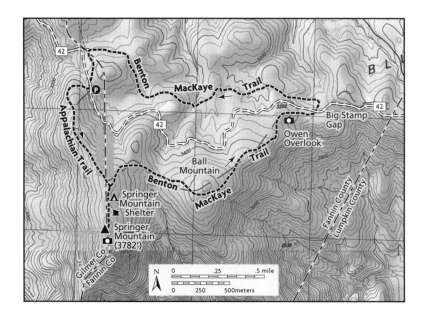

Glenn and Susan Schuffenhauer take a break at the start of the Appalachian Trail at Springer Mountain.

in the winter months at one of the two bronze plaques at the summit. The first plaque is secured into a rock outcropping that has excellent views to the west. This original plaque has marked the southern terminus of the Appalachian Trail since 1958 when it was moved to Springer Mountain from nearby Mount Oglethorpe. The second, larger plaque, dedicated in 1993, sits atop a partially man-made, trunk-sized boulder, with a metal box at the base. There may be a spiral notebook and pen in this container where modern-day adventurers swap stories and long-distance thru-hikers mark the beginning or end of their journey.

At the parking area off Forest Road 42, cross back over the gravel road and begin a moderate ascent toward Springer Mountain, following the white blazes of the Appalachian Trail (AT) on this loop hike. After 0.7 mile, the trail meets with the Benton MacKaye Trail (BMT) on the left, marked with white diamonds. Continue south on the AT and ascend slightly to reach the summit of Springer Mountain. You will pass another side trail on the left marked with blue blazes after 20 feet. It leads to several campsites and the two-story Springer Mountain Shelter. For those who plan to make this an overnight adventure, the blue-blazed side trail leads to the best campsites on the route. There is water near the shelter at a small spring, which occasionally runs dry in the late summer months. Otherwise, continue for another 0.2 mile to reach Springer Mountain and the southern terminus of the Appalachian Trail.

Bismarck sports some winter-wear in anticipation of a cool night on the trail.

After enjoying the views at Springer, retrace your steps on the Appalachian Trail and follow the white rectangular blazes. As the trail forks, leave the AT and follow the white diamonds to the right and northeast on the Benton MacKaye Trail. The hike will come to another blue-blazed side trail after walking 1.5 miles on the Benton MacKaye Trail. It leads about 50 yards to a small hillside clearing called the Owen Overlook with some spectacular views of the surrounding valley. This is an excellent opportunity for you and the dog to take a break and enjoy the views to the north.

The route continues on the Benton MacKaye Trail and descends gradually to reach Big Stamp Gap, where the trail crosses the gravel Forest Road 42 and begins heading west. The hike continues over the road and follows the Benton MacKaye Trail 1.5 miles through laurel and rhododendron. It then crosses several small streams before the trail again intersects with the Appalachian Trail. At this junction, the hike turns left onto the AT and returns to the parking lot at Forest Road 42.

The Benton MacKaye Trail is less traveled and more peaceful than the AT. The Springer Mountain area is very popular, however, particularly on weekends. There will be many hikers and backpackers in this area, so keep pets on a leash while taking a break at Springer Mountain. Overnight backpackers will find plenty of campsites in and around the Springer Mountain Shelter if they wish to camp for the night.

10. DeSoto Falls

Round trip: 1.9 miles
Difficulty: Easy to moderate
Hiking time: 1 hour
High point: 2370 feet
Elevation gain: 334 feet
Best season: Spring, summer, fall
Map: USGS Neels Gap Quad
Fees and permits: Parking fee, campground fee
Contact: Chattahoochee National Forest, Brasstown Ranger
    District, P.O. Box 9, Blairsville, GA 30512, (706) 745-6928,
    www.fs.fed.us/conf

Getting there: (From Atlanta, GA, 1.5 hours; from Dahlonega, GA, 30 minutes) In Dahlonega, take US 19 for approximately 12.5 miles to its junction with US 129 at Turners Corner. At this intersection, turn right and continue on US 129 north for about 4 miles. Turn left at the DeSoto Falls Recreation Area sign for access to the trailhead and campground.

The falls and the surrounding scenic area were named for Hernando DeSoto, a Spanish explorer who was known to have traveled the wilderness in search of gold. Early settlers found a piece of armor here, and suddenly a mountain legend was born. It was believed that DeSoto and his men left the armor behind as they explored the Southeast for treasure. Unfortunately for DeSoto, he and his followers were searching in the wrong place. In the 1830s, not far from this location, there was a gold rush that is well documented in a museum at the center of town in nearby Dahlonega, Georgia.

DeSoto Falls Recreation and Scenic Area consists of both a campground and a well-maintained hiking trail to two waterfalls on Frogtown Creek.

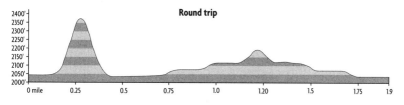

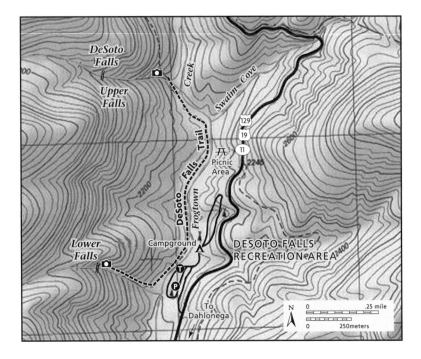

The falls are close to the parking area (Lower and Upper Falls), are easily accessed, and are a very worthwhile destination for backcountry hikers.

The in-and-out hike begins across the bridge over Frogtown Creek and follows the stream to both the Lower and Upper waterfalls. To access the Lower Falls, follow the trail southbound for approximately 0.5 mile. To access the Upper Falls, hike from the Lower Falls, pass the trailhead again on your right, then continue northbound for another 0.45 mile, following the signs to the Upper Falls. Both cascades have viewing platforms that provide a perfect opportunity for you and your dog to take a break. Here you can enjoy a forest that was once cherished by the Cherokee Indians, and hikers can relax and listen to the peaceful sounds of a rolling mountain stream. Lower Falls drops approximately 30 feet, but Upper Falls is more dramatic with an impressive 90-foot plunge to a small pool at its base. Dogs will enjoy wallowing in these shallow pools and appreciate the cool shade near the viewing platforms.

It is worth noting that older maps list three falls in the DeSoto Falls Recreation Area: Lower, Middle, and Upper Falls. The Chattahoochee National Forest has renamed the Middle Falls as the Upper Falls and closed the trail to the cascade marked as "Upper Falls" on older topographical maps. This

Upper DeSoto Falls as viewed from the wooden platform at the base of the waterfall

is for safety reasons, so follow their guidance and stick to the trail.

For those looking for an overnight adventure, there is no backcountry camping in the DeSoto Falls Recreation Area. Most visitors stay in the twenty-four drive-in campsites near the trailhead, which require self-registration and a camping fee. These sites are only open from mid-April through October. Warm showers, flush toilets, and potable water are provided in the campground, and each site has a tent pad, picnic table, fire ring, and lantern pole. Dogs are allowed in the DeSoto Falls Recreation Area, but must be on a leash at both the campground and on the trail.

11. Black Rock Mountain

Round trip: 2.2 miles
Difficulty: Moderate
Hiking time: 1 hour
High point: 3640 feet
Elevation gain: 420 feet
Best season: Any season
Maps: Black Rock Mountain State Park; USGS Dillard Quad
Contact: Black Rock Mountain State Park, P.O. Drawer A,
    Mountain City, GA, 30562, (706) 746-2141,
    www.gastateparks.org/info/blackrock

Getting there: (From Greenville, SC, 1.5 hours; from Clayton, GA, 5 minutes) From US 76 and 441 in Clayton, GA, drive 3 miles north on US 441 to the Black Mountain Parkway. Look for the brown directional signs for Black Rock Mountain State Park in Mountain City. Take the Black Rock Mountain Parkway and follow the signs to the state park's visitor center, on the left. The trailhead is located on the right before you reach the Blue Ridge overlook.

Black Rock Mountain State Park is named for the sheer cliffs of dark-colored rock found occasionally in Georgia's Blue Ridge Mountains. The park is located on both sides of the Eastern Continental Divide at an altitude of 3640 feet, and Black Rock Mountain is the highest state park in Georgia. Hikers will enjoy dramatic views of the Southern Appalachians, and several hiking trails lead visitors past cascading streams and waterfalls in the park.

The Tennessee Rock Trail is an ideal day hike for both hikers and their dogs, and it contains some of the most spectacular vistas in the park. The trail is challenging enough to provide some exercise, but not too

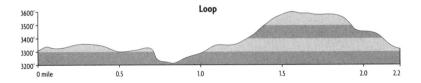

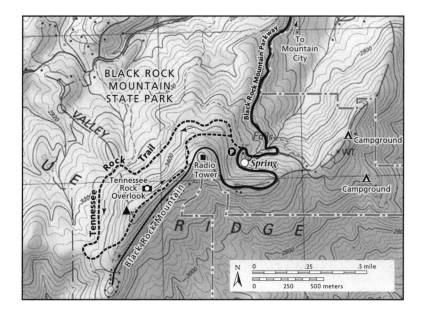

steep to exhaust both you and your pooch. Drinking water is available from the public source at the visitor center, where you can also pick up a park map.

The yellow-blazed Tennessee Rock Trail leaves the parking lot and passes a picnic area before the path disappears into a forested habitat. Winding southwest, the trail gently ascends and descends along the northwestern side of Black Rock Mountain where there are excellent views down toward Clayton, Georgia.

After about 1 mile, the Tennessee Rock Trail begins a hairpin turn as it loops back to the northeast. It then begins a 200-foot ascent up to the summit of Black Rock Mountain, which in the winter months has spectacular views of the surrounding mountains.

From the summit, the trail follows the spine of Black Rock Mountain until reaching Tennessee Rock, the trail's namesake. From this vantage point hikers can see range after range of the southern Appalachians, including Clingman's Dome in the Great Smoky Mountains National Park. Beyond Tennessee Rock, the trail hugs the parkway and winds around a small knob on the way back to the parking area.

For those looking for an overnight adventure, there are no campsites along this trail. However, Black Rock Mountain State Park has two primitive campsites and a campground with forty-eight drive-in sites. There are

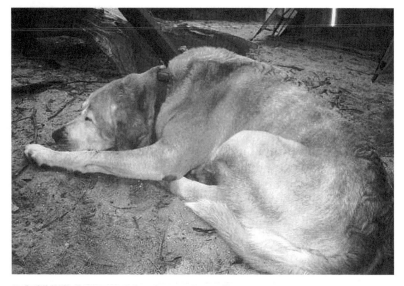

Rebel rests after an exciting day on the trail.

also ten cottages for rent, and two of the cabins are now "dog-friendly." Advance reservations are required.

The 17-acre Black Rock Lake is nearby and is open year-round to all visitors. Fishing is restricted to the banks of the lake, but a trout stamp is not required. Anglers will find bass, bluegill, catfish, and trout in the water. For hikers, the park also has a new 0.85-mile forest path that encircles the lake, perfect for a leisurely stroll with the dog.

12. Rabun Bald

Round trip: 8.4 miles
Difficulty: Moderate to difficult
Hiking time: 4–6 hours
High point: 4696 feet
Elevation gain/loss: 1446 feet
Best season: Any season
Map: USGS Rabun Bald Quad
Contact: Chattahoochee National Forest, Tallulah Ranger District, 809 Highway 441 South, Clayton, GA 30525, (706) 782-3320, *www.fs.fed.us/conf*

Getting there: (From Atlanta, GA, 2 hours; from Greenville, SC, 2 hours) In Clayton, Georgia, start at the junction of US 76 and 441, and head north for 8.0 miles. Before you reach the North Carolina border, turn right onto Route 246. Here there is a sign pointing toward Sky Valley, and Route 246 becomes Route 106 as you enter North Carolina. Drive 4.3 miles and pass Old Mud Creek Road on the right. (Note: This is the turn-off for Beegum Gap and Rabun Gap.) Continue on Route 106 to the town of Scaly Mountain. At the ski lifts (and before you reach the post office), turn right onto Bald Mountain Road. Follow Bald Mountain Road for 2.1 miles until the road forks, then turn left onto a gravel road that is Hale Ridge Road. Follow Hale Ridge Road for 1.1 miles to an intersection with the Bartram Trail. There is a parking area here large enough for a few cars.

This in-and-out hike starts at Hale Ridge Road and follows the Bartram Trail south to Rabun Bald with an elevation of 4696 feet. The Bartram Trail is named after William Bartram (1739–1823), an American naturalist who explored and documented the flora and fauna in several Southern states during Colonial times. The footpath named in his honor follows the route that the explorer used as he recorded and cataloged over 200 species of native plants in the Southeast.

To start the hike, leave Hale Ridge Road and hike southwest for the first few miles on the yellow-blazed Bartram Trail, wandering past a small waterfall after 0.3 mile and over a series of modest streams. Overnight backpackers should note that there are some potential campsites in this area, although the best sites are located on and around Rabun Bald. Load up on water now, since there is none available at the summit.

At 2.6 miles, you'll reach Beegum Gap, a confusing area with some dirt roads, houses, and mountain cottages scattered along the Bartram Trail. Be sure to follow the yellow blazes carefully and keep your dog on a leash; the neighbors will appreciate it. (Note: Kelsey Mountain Road can be reached by turning right from the Bartram Trail onto the dirt road at Beegum Gap. This trailhead cuts over 5 miles off this in-and-out hike if an easier route is desired.)

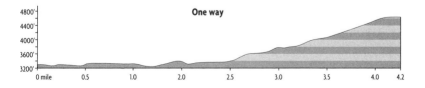

Leaving Beegum Gap, the Bartram Trail ascends steeply for about 1200 feet over the next 1.2 miles. Until now there has been only 200 feet of elevation change, but things are about to get much tougher. So take your time, and rest up at Rabun Gap, which is only about 0.5 mile from Rabun Bald. The break will make the pooch much happier, and the final push to the summit will be much more enjoyable.

After 4.2 miles, the Bartram Trail finally reaches the summit of Rabun Bald. The stone lookout tower comes into view on the left as you close in on the peak. After Brasstown Bald it is the second-highest mountain in Georgia, and there are spectacular 360-degree views from the flat platform fixed to the base of the tower. Hikers can see the states of Georgia,

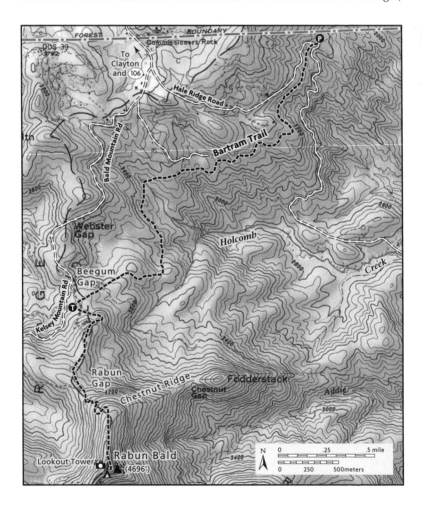

Morning clouds lie in the valley floor after a rainy night on Rabun Bald.

North Carolina, and South Carolina from the remodeled observation tower, and on the Fourth of July hikers may witness fireworks from three neighboring communities.

The fantastic views make Rabun Bald an attractive overnight destination for backpackers, but a word of caution is in order—especially for the hot, humid summer months. Rabun Bald is prone to strong thunder and lightning storms, and the exposed summit is extremely dangerous in these conditions. Most dogs are spooked by thunder, so plan accordingly. There are some small campsites along the Bartram Trail just south of the summit. They are tucked in the trees and are much safer than the open area around the tower. Both day hikers and overnight backpackers should watch for dark clouds in the skies to the south or southwest and get off Rabun Bald well before a storm hits. It is also recommended that all pets be on a leash around the summit, since it is a popular day-hiking destination for many people who live in the area.

CENTRAL/ SOUTHERN GEORGIA

13. Lake Allatoona

Round trip: 5.5 miles
Difficulty: Easy
Hiking time: 2.5 hours
High point: 1000 feet
Elevation gain: 150 feet
Best season: Any season
Maps: Red Top Mountain State Park; USGS Allatoona Dam Quad
Contact: Red Top Mountain State Park, 781 Red Top Mountain
    Road SE, Cartersville, GA 30120, (770) 975-4226,
    www.gastateparkes.org/info/redtop

Getting there: (From Atlanta, GA, 45 minutes) In Atlanta, take I-75 north to Exit 123 (Red Top Mountain Road). Travel east on Red Top Mountain Road for approximately 1 mile to the Red Top Mountain State Park entrance. Park at the visitor center, where you can pick up a trail map.

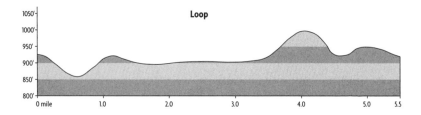

Lake Allatoona, located just northwest of Atlanta, is a popular boating destination in the state. Hikers, however, will enjoy exploring the lake by the Homestead Loop Trail. The 5.5-mile trail is located in Red Top Mountain State Park. Red Top Mountain (in the northwestern corner of the park) got its name from the high iron-ore content in the resident soil. The mountain was once an important mining area for the metal, but today is largely appreciated for its easy access to 12,000-acre Lake Allatoona and for offering a respite from the urban life in nearby Atlanta.

The Homestead Loop Trail starts at the park's visitor center and occasionally hugs the banks of Lake Allatoona as it winds through some of the most diverse habitats of all the trails in the park. The ecosystems include lake, forest, and meadow areas for wildlife that thrive in the

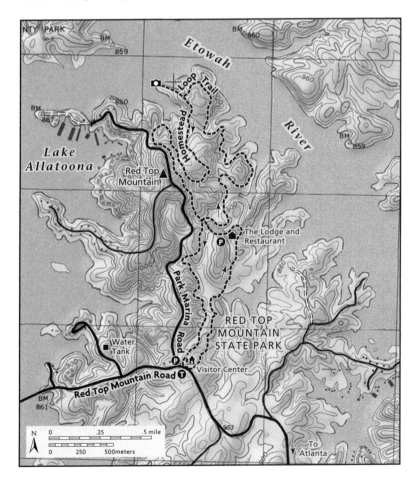

Rob Schwartz walks his dog Max along the shores of Lake Allatoona.

region. The overabundant population has caused the Department of Natural Resources and the University of Georgia to team up to study and recommend a management approach to ensure a healthy environment for the entire ecosystem.

From the parking area, follow the yellow blazes of the Homestead Loop north from the visitor center. After about 2 miles, the trail passes the Red Top Mountain Lodge to the left. It has thirty-three rooms that can be reserved in advance, although pets are not allowed in or around the lodge. The hike continues across Lodge Road, and the Homestead Loop (if traveled counterclockwise) follows the edge of Lake Allatoona for the first 2.5 miles with excellent views to the northeast.

As the trail turns toward the southwest, there is a blue-blazed side trail that leads to a small peninsula with 270-degree views of the lake. It is well worth the effort, particularly at dusk.

After backtracking from the vista, continue along the yellow-blazed trail as it heads inland past Red Top Mountain and along the Marina Road. Eventually, the route leads back to the visitor center, although it is possible to cut the distance in half on this loop by starting the hike at the lodge.

The Homestead Loop is easily traveled and makes for a pleasant day hike. Dogs will enjoy swimming in the lake, so this hike is particularly suited for the warmer months (but it is enjoyable year-round). Red Top Mountain State Park does not permit backcountry camping, but has eighteen cottages, ninety-two campsites, and even a yurt for overnight use. Pets are allowed at the campsites but not at the cottages, lodge, or yurt. The park service also asks that dogs be leashed at all times and that owners clean up after them.

14. Sweetwater Creek

Round trip: 4.2 miles
Difficulty: Easy to moderate
Hiking time: 1.5 hours
High point: 1025 feet
Elevation gain: 225 feet
Best season: Spring, fall, winter
Maps: Sweetwater Creek State Park; USGS Austell Quad
Contact: Sweetwater Creek State Conservation Park, Lithia Springs, GA 30122, (770) 732-5871, *www.gastateparks.org/info/sweetwater*

Getting there: (From Atlanta, GA, 15 minutes) In Atlanta, take I-20 west to Exit 44 (Thornton Road). Turn left and continue 0.25 mile. Turn right onto Blairs Bridge Road and continue 2 miles. Turn left onto Mount Vernon Road. Sweetwater Creek State Park is on the left. Once you enter the park, continue 0.5 mile and turn onto Factory Shoals Road. The parking lot for the trailhead is at the end of the road. You can pick up a map here or download one from Georgia State Parks website.

Sweetwater Creek State Park has over 9 miles of hiking trails and is located only a short distance from downtown Atlanta. The Sweetwater Creek Conservation Park was created to preserve the unique natural and cultural

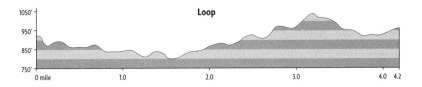

history of the area, which includes the ruins of the New Manchester Manufacturing Company. The old textile mill sits along Sweetwater Creek and is visible on this loop hike. General Sherman burned it to the ground in July 1864 since it once made clothing for the Confederate troops during the Civil War (or "War Between the States," as it is sometimes referred to in the South). Along the creek, which more closely resembles a river, there are numerous viewpoints, including one at Sweetwater Falls located at the junction of the Red and White Trails.

This loop hike begins by following the red blazes of the Red Trail (also known as the History Trail). After about 0.5 mile, the path reaches the mill ruins at Sweetwater Creek. The trail travels through the "main street" area of the old town of New Manchester and also traverses the site of the old town store, the dam, and the mill itself.

The Red Trail is the most frequently used path in the park due to its proximity to the mill and because of the scenic Sweetwater Creek. For

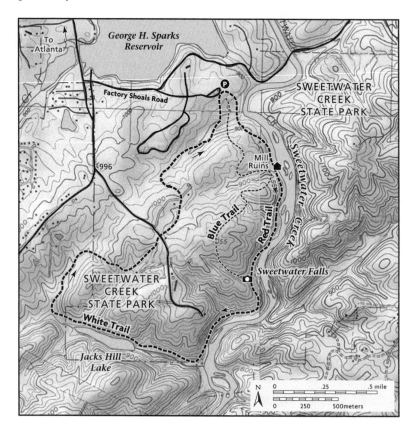

Charlie and Katie Brady head out with Rebel on the Red Trail at Sweetwater Creek State Park.

this reason, the park requires that pets be leashed at all times. In contrast, the White Trail (also known as the Non-Game Wildlife Trail) is less used and more peaceful, albeit less scenic.

At Sweetwater Falls, pick up the White Trail and turn away from Sweetwater Creek along Jacks Hill Creek. During a gradual ascent, Jacks Hill Lake quickly comes into view down an embankment to the left. Here there are often turtles sunning themselves on the rocks and stumps in the lake. The White Trail continues gaining altitude as it leaves the lake and reaches a pretty meadow area with flowers blooming during the warmer months. The hound may want a sniff of these wildflowers before you move on. From the meadow (sometimes known as Jacks Hill Meadow), the White Trail traverses a picnic area, then returns to the parking area where the hike began.

Sweetwater Creek State Park is a day-use facility, and there are not currently any overnight facilities for hikers and backpackers. Eleven picnic shelters and one group shelter are available for day use, however.

15. Buzzard Roost

Round trip: 8.3 miles
Difficulty: Moderate to difficult
Hiking time: 4–5 hours
High point: 1338 feet
Elevation gain: 475 feet
Best season: Any season
Map: Pine Mountain Trail Association map
Contact: Franklin D. Roosevelt State Park, 2970 Georgia Highway
190, Pine Mountain, GA 31822, (706) 663-4858,
www.gastateparks.org/info/fdr

Getting there: (From Atlanta, GA, 1.25 hours; from Columbus, GA, 30
minutes) In Atlanta, take I-85 south toward Montgomery for 47.3 miles
to Exit 21, I-185 toward Columbus/Fort Benning. (Note: The last good
chance for fast food and groceries is at Exit 47 off I-85 at Newnan. Take
a left off the exit ramp for several fast-food places and a grocery superstore.) You will only be on I-185 a few miles to Exit 42 and US 27 south
(5.9 miles from the start of the off-ramp off I-85 to the off-ramp at Exit
42). Take a left at the end of the Exit 42 off-ramp, and head toward Pine
Mountain. Pass through Pine Mountain on US 27 south to a traffic light
at Route 354 (10.5 miles from I-185). Take a left onto Route 354.

Stay on Route 354 for another 2.6 miles until you see an off-ramp to your
right and signs for Route 190. If you go under a stone bridge, you have
gone too far! Turn right onto Route 190, and drive 0.4 mile down Route
190 to reach the Franklin D. Roosevelt State Park office and visitor center
(a big stone building on the left), an alternate start/end point for this hike
if more convenient. There are two parking areas here, a loop on the left of
the building, and another smaller area on the right. It is 1 mile from the
FDR State Park office to the parking lot and trailhead on Route 190, located
just southeast of Indian Mountain and north of Fox Den Cove.

The Pine Mountain Trail is a 23-mile footpath that crosses and follows
Pine Mountain Ridge in west-central Georgia. The trail is inside Franklin
Delano Roosevelt State Park, close to Calloway Gardens, and popular
with people from all over the state. Much of the land in the park once

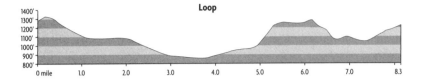

belonged to President Franklin D. Roosevelt, whose farm was located near the present site of WJSP-TV. Today, volunteers from the Pine Mountain Trail Association maintain the path, which includes many points of interest and very few steep inclines. The association's trail map is sold by FDR State Park and available at the office/visitor center. The trail was first developed in 1975 and now is used by over 50,000 hikers and backpackers each year.

Buzzard Roost is an overlook located along a ridge in the park, and this 8-mile loop hike combines a section of the Pine Mountain Trail with parts of two smaller loop trails: Long Leaf and the Mountain Creek Nature Trail Loops. This is one of four hikes featured in Franklin D. Roosevelt State Park (see also Hikes 16, 17, and 18) and is the westernmost of the routes, with an option of starting at the park office, the campground, or a trailhead to the east. This book profiles a counterclockwise route beginning at the Route 190 parking area between miles 6 and 7 of the Pine Mountain Trail.

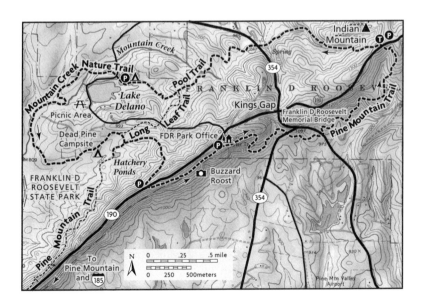

The visitor center at Franklin D. Roosevelt State Park

Start by hiking northwest on the Pine Mountain Trail for 0.5 mile to where it intersects with the white-blazed Pool Trail. After 1.2 miles, leash the pooch and carefully cross Route 354, a secondary road running north-and-south through the park. Ascend gradually from here to a small knob at around 1050 feet. The terrain stays close to this elevation for about 1 mile, then begins a gentle descent down and past some campgrounds located at Lake Delano.

The 15-acre lake was dug by hand by CCC workers using very little machinery. This gave jobs to Depression-era workers during a period of great economic unrest in the United States. Dogs will enjoy the fruits of this labor, since there is no shortage of water at Lake Delano. Hikers will also enjoy the other outdoor activities here, including fishing, boating, and camping (an alternative to the Dead Pine Campsite, a backcountry destination about 4 miles into the hike).

Watch the trail and red blazes carefully at Lake Delano to pick up the Mountain Creek Nature Trail, especially if you plan to camp at the Dead Pine Campsite. Crystal Branch is the water source for the backcountry site, so keep the dog out of the water and walk a short distance from here to rejoin with the Pine Mountain Trail.

After the Dead Pine Campsite, the trail heads south briefly, then rejoins the Pine Mountain Trail to make a hairpin turn and head back to the east toward Buzzard Roost. The overlook is located on the southern slopes of the state park, and after the 300-foot climb the pooch will likely enjoy a short break. The state park office is only a brief walk to the east from Buzzard Roost, and a short side trail leads to the facility if fresh water or a rest room break is needed. The park office also makes a great starting or ending point for this loop hike if it is more convenient. Check inside the office for a backcountry map of the Pine Mountain Trail.

The final few miles of the Buzzard Roost hike continue along the southern ridge of the park, heading east to cross Route 354 again. Then the trail gradually winds to the northeast to finish at the starting point off Route 190.

Both day hikers and overnight backpackers will enjoy this moderately difficult route through Franklin D. Roosevelt State Park, and will understand why FDR spent so much time in this area until his death on April 12, 1945.

16. Lil' Butt Knob

Round trip: 8.8 miles
Difficulty: Moderate to difficult
Hiking time: 5 hours
High point: 1330 feet
Elevation gain: 330 feet
Best season: Any season
Map: Pine Mountain Trail Association
Contact: Franklin D. Roosevelt State Park, 2970 Georgia Highway
190, Pine Mountain, GA 31822, (706) 663-4858,
www.gastateparks.org/info/fdr

Getting there: (From Atlanta, GA, 1.25 hours; from Columbus, GA, 30 minutes) In Atlanta, take I-85 south toward Montgomery for 47.3 miles

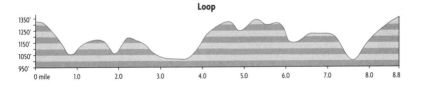

to Exit 21, I-185 toward Columbus/Fort Benning. (Note: The last good chance for fast food and groceries is at Exit 47 off I-85 at Newnan. Take a left off the exit ramp for several fast-food places and a grocery superstore.) You will only be on I-185 a few miles to Exit 42 and US 27 south (5.9 miles from the start of the off-ramp off I-85 to the off-ramp at Exit 42). Take a left at the end of the Exit 42 off-ramp, and head toward Pine Mountain. Pass through Pine Mountain on US 27 south to a traffic light at Route 354 (10.5 miles from I-185). Take a left onto Route 354.

Stay on Route 354 for another 2.6 miles until you see an off-ramp to your right and signs for Route 190. If you go under a stone bridge, you have gone too far! Turn right onto Route 190, and drive 0.4 mile down Route 190 to reach the Franklin D. Roosevelt State Park office and visitor center (a big stone building on the left); there are two parking areas here, a loop on the left of the building, and another smaller area on the right. From the FDR State Park office/visitor center, head east on Route 190 for 3 miles to the Pine Mountain Trail at mile 11, where there is a small parking lot on the side of the road.

The Lil' Butt Knob hike is one of four loop trails that utilize a portion of the Pine Mountain Trail in Franklin D. Roosevelt State Park (see Hike 15 for more information about the Pine Mountain Trail and the state park). The Lil' Butt Knob route is suitable for either day or overnight hiking, with three designated campsites along the route at Beech Bottom, Big Knot, and Grindstone Campsites.

This trail description starts near mile 11 on the Pine Mountain Trail,

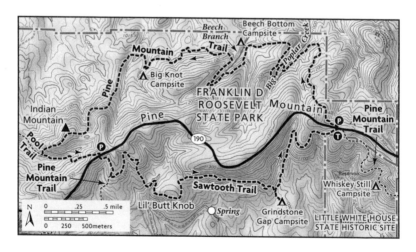

where it crosses Route 190 and follows the blue blazes in a counterclockwise direction just west of Hines Gap. Heading northwest, hike around the eastern side of a small knob at 1343 feet, then make a gradual 200-foot descent to Big Poplar Creek, a possible water source. Here the trail makes a series of hairpin turns around the stream before gaining elevation again to cross a small ridge. The ridge separates the Big Poplar and Beech Branch drainages.

There is a nice campsite at Beech Bottom situated a short distance off the trail, with water usually available from the stream. A second designated backcountry area known as Big Knot Campsite can be found a mile past Rattlesnake Bluff. Both offer rustic accommodations for backcountry hikers and their pets. The dog should take a healthy drink in this area, since there are no other reliable water sources on the remainder of the route.

Leaving Big Knot Campsite, the blue-blazed Pine Mountain Trail heads southwest, crosses Indian Mountain at 1330 feet, and meets the white-blazed Pool Trail after 4.4 miles (marking the ceremonial halfway point on this loop hike). High-five your canine, then continue following the white blazes past Fox Den Cove, turning southeast and crossing Route 190 after 4.9 miles. (and an alternative parking area and starting point for this loop hike). Watch the pooch carefully in this area since motorists do occasionally speed through here. After 5.1 miles, the Pine

Views to the southeast from Dowdell Knob in Franklin D. Roosevelt State Park

Mountain Trail meets the white-blazed Sawtooth Trail, the return route to the trailhead.

Follow the Sawtooth Trail, turning east, and ascend Lil' Butt Knob (1200 feet) which has winter views to the south, looking down toward Lake Franklin. From the knob, traverse the hillside with only a slight elevation change for roughly 0.5 mile. Then make a gradual descent to the Grindstone Gap Campsite (also a short distance off the trail). This is the last opportunity for your pet to take a break before the Sawtooth Trail makes an abrupt turn and heads northeast back to the trailhead at Route 190.

17. Sunset Rock

Round trip: 11.4 miles
Difficulty: Moderate to difficult
Hiking time: 6–7 hours
High point: 1300 feet
Elevation gain: 230 feet
Best season: Any season
Map: Pine Mountain Trail Association map
Contact: Franklin D. Roosevelt State Park, 2970 Georgia Highway
    190, Pine Mountain, GA 31822, (706) 663-4858,
    www.gastateparks.org/info/fdr

Getting there: (From Atlanta, GA, 1.25 hours; from Columbus, GA, 30 minutes) In Atlanta, take I-85 south toward Montgomery for 47.3 miles to Exit 21, I-185 toward Columbus/Fort Benning. (Note: The last good chance for fast food and groceries is at Exit 47 off I-85 at Newnan. Take a left off the exit ramp for several fast-food places and a grocery super- store.) You will only be on I-185 a few miles to Exit 42 and US 27 south (5.9 miles from the start of the off-ramp off I-85 to the off-ramp at Exit 42). Take a left at the end of the Exit 42 off-ramp, and head toward Pine

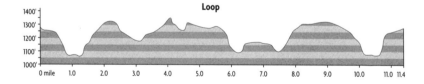

Mountain. Pass through Pine Mountain on US 27 south to a traffic light at Route 354 (10.5 miles from I-185). Take a left onto Route 354.

Stay on Route 354 for another 2.6 miles until you see an off-ramp to your right and signs for Route 190. If you go under a stone bridge, you have gone too far! Turn right onto Route 190, and drive 0.4 mile down Route 190 to reach the Franklin D. Roosevelt State Park office and visitor center (a big stone building on the left); there are two parking areas here, a loop on the left of the building, and another smaller area on the right. It is 6.4 miles from the FDR State Park office on Route 190 to the Rocky Point trailhead and parking area at mile 18 on the Pine Mountain Trail.

The Sunset Rock hike is one of four loop trails in this book that utilize a portion of the Pine Mountain Trail in Franklin D. Roosevelt State Park (see Hike 15 for more information about the Pine Mountain Trail and the state park). The Sunset Rock route, at 11.4 miles, is the longest of the Pine Mountain Trail loop hikes. The loop can be hiked either direction, but we follow it here headed clockwise from the parking area.

Begin at the Rocky Point trailhead on the blue-blazed Pine Mountain Trail, near mile 18, and descend gradually southwest to the Sparks Creek Campsite. About 0.5 mile past the campsite, the Pine Mountain Trail intersects with the white-blazed Boottop Trail. Bear left and follow the blue blazes of the Pine Mountain Trail another 2 miles, climbing gradually until you reach a clearing with some facilities known as Dowdell Knob.

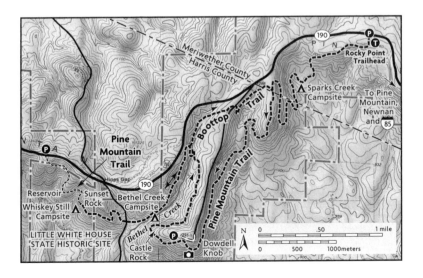

Watching the very last rays of sunshine from Sunset Rock near the Whiskey Still Campsite

This makes a perfect rest stop, and you and the dog may even be able to "Yogi" a few treats from the picnickers—particularly on weekends.

Dowdell Knob, located about halfway through the loop, is the highlight of the route, with 180-degree views sweeping from the southeast to the southwest. It is accessible by vehicle with paved roads and picnic tables, but for hikers and backpackers, it is an opportunity to enjoy the best views in the park. Unlike many high points on the Pine Mountain Trail, however, the views at Dowdell Knob are available year-round and are well worth the effort.

From Dowdell Knob, the trail turns sharply northwest toward Castle Rock. It then completes the boot-shaped circumnavigation of Dowdell Knob with a turn to the northeast to intersect again with the Boottop Trail at Bethel Creek.

From here it is a 1-mile in-and-out hike to Sunset Rock. The Bethel Creek Campsite is only a short distance southwest from this junction. Overnight backpackers can reserve this site or push on farther west to the Whiskey Still Campsite, a smaller backcountry site with only three tent sites. Water is available from a spring 0.4 mile down the valley. Backcountry permits are required for all campsites, and no more than fifteen people are allowed to use them at any given time.

Sunset Rock is situated along a south-facing ridge between the Bethel Creek and Whiskey Still Campsites and has winter views to the southwest. Campers often enjoy the view at dusk from a small outcropping near the trail. Dowdell Knob has more sweeping views, but Sunset Rock also looks west and has significantly more solitude and an overnight backcountry site (Whiskey Still) only a short distance away.

For those who prefer more amenities, there is a campground nearby with 140 drive-in sites. It is a short distance from the Pine Mountain Trail, but still in the boundaries of Franklin D. Roosevelt State Park. Pets are allowed on the Pine Mountain Trail and at the campground as long as they are on a leash of no longer than six feet.

Hikers and backpackers will backtrack to the Boottop Trail to complete this loop hike and can knock 2 miles off the route by skipping the side hike to Sunset Rock. This option may be particularly appealing to day hikers who do not plan to stay in the backcountry overnight.

18. The Wolfden

Round trip: 6.7 miles
Difficulty: Easy to moderate
Hiking time: 3 hours
High point: 1300 feet
Elevation gain: 300 feet
Best season: Any season
Map: Pine Mountain Trail Association map
Contact: Franklin D. Roosevelt State Park, 2970 Georgia Highway 190, Pine Mountain, GA 31822, (706) 663-4858, *www.gastateparks.org/info/fdr*

Getting there: (From Atlanta, GA, 1.25 hours; from Columbus, GA, 30 minutes) In Atlanta, take I-85 south toward Montgomery for 47.3 miles to Exit 21, I-185 toward Columbus/Fort Benning. (Note: The last good chance for fast food and groceries is at Exit 47 off I-85 at Newnan. Take a left off the exit ramp for several fast-food places and a grocery superstore.)

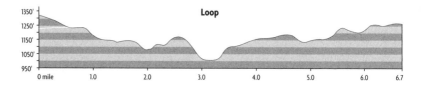

You will only be on I-185 a few miles to Exit 42 and US 27 south (5.9 miles from the start of the off-ramp from I-85 to the off-ramp at Exit 42). Take a left at the end of the Exit 42 off-ramp, and head toward Pine Mountain. Pass through Pine Mountain on US 27 south to a traffic light at Route 354 (10.5 miles from I-185). Take a left onto Route 354.

Stay on Route 354 for another 2.6 miles until you see an off-ramp to your right and signs for Route 190. If you go under a stone bridge, you have gone too far! Turn right onto Route 190, and drive 0.4 mile down Route 190 to reach the Franklin D. Roosevelt State Park office and visitor center (a big stone building on the left); there are two parking areas here, a loop on the

The Wolfden, a cave just to the east of the Pine Mountain Trail

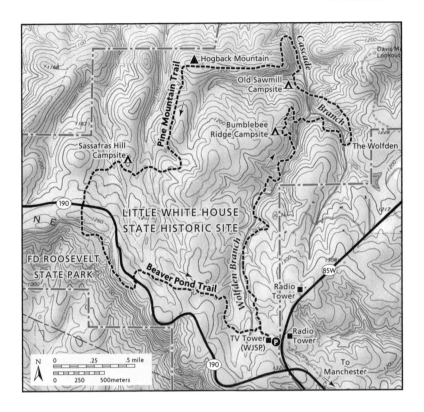

left of the building, and another smaller area on the right. The trailhead is 8.5 miles east from the FDR State Park office on Route 190.

The Wolfden is one of four loop trails that utilize a portion of the Pine Mountain Trail in Franklin D. Roosevelt State Park (see Hike 15 for more information about the Pine Mountain Trail and the state park). This is the easternmost of the loop hikes and starts at the WJSP-TV tower, which sits at the eastern terminus of the Pine Mountain Trail.

This 6.7-mile loop hike leaves the parking area and follows the blue blazes of the Pine Mountain Trail north in a counterclockwise direction. Along the first leg of the loop, which closely follows the Wolfden Branch, there are several small but beautiful waterfalls, including Dry Falls, Csonka Falls, Big Rock Falls, Slippery Rock Falls, and Cascade Falls. Each provides an excellent opportunity to enjoy the lovely mountain scenery that Franklin D. Roosevelt (more commonly known as FDR) so cherished in the area.

As the hike continues, the trail passes the Bumblebee Ridge and Old Sawmill Campsites. Sandwiched between them is The Wolfden, an interesting cave-like structure, just to the right of the trail and certainly worth some extra time to explore or photograph. The pooch is likely to catch the smells of local wildlife that dwell in this area, and quite possibly within the small cave or along the Cascade Branch drainage. Raccoons, skunks, porcupines, and foxes are all common in Franklin D. Roosevelt State Park.

At The Wolfden, the trail turns northwest and follows the Cascade Branch until it makes a hairpin turn and ascends to Hogback Mountain at just over 1200 feet. A short distance past the mountain is the Sassafras Hill Campsite, just off the trail to the north on a small knob. It sits between the Bettie Branch and Mount Hope Branch drainages and is the last of the three campsites along this section of trail.

Overnight backpackers should check at the park office for a permit for any of the backcountry sites. Water is more reliable along the Cascade and Wolfden Branches, so load up there before staying at Sassafras Hill Campsite.

To return to the WJSP-TV parking area, pick up the white-blazed Beaver Pond Trail, located at mile 18. Turn southeast off the Pine Mountain Trail and follow the Beaver Pond Trail across Route 190 for the final 1.7 miles to return to the starting point.

19. Beaver Trail

Round trip: 1.2 miles
Difficulty: Easy
Hiking time: 1 hour
High point: 225 feet
Elevation gain: Negligible
Best season: Any season
Map: USGS Millen Quad
Contact: Magnolia Springs State Park, 1053 Magnolia Springs Drive, Millen, GA 30442, (478) 982-1660

Getting there: (From Atlanta, GA, 3.25 hours; from Savannah, GA, 2 hours) In Atlanta, take I-20 east toward Augusta. Merge onto I-520 east and travel 7 miles to Exit 7 (Windsor Springs/Peach Orchard Road). Take

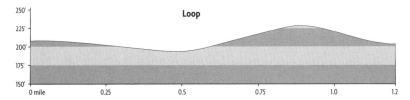

the I-520 east ramp, turn right onto US 25 south, and drive 23 miles. Turn right again onto US 25 for another 14 miles. Due to road construction on US 25, the original park entrance is no longer in existence, so drive past Magnolia Springs Road to the top of the hill and turn left onto Lawton Road, a county road, then take an immediate left on the new park entrance drive that parallels US 25. Park by the lake near the boat dock.

Magnolia Springs State Park is known for its crystal-clear springs from which seven to nine million gallons of water flow each day into the lake systems of the park. A boardwalk spans this crisp, cool water. The reliable water source led the Confederate Army to use this site during the Civil War as a prison camp for nearly 40,000 Union soldiers. The earthen breastworks of Fort Lawton, built to defend the prison stockade, can still be seen by park visitors. Archaeological surveys are underway, and a museum in Group Shelter 1 contains information on Camp Lawton. Nearby is the Millen National Fish Hatchery, which is no longer operational,

Rebel relaxes after a refreshing swim in the lake.

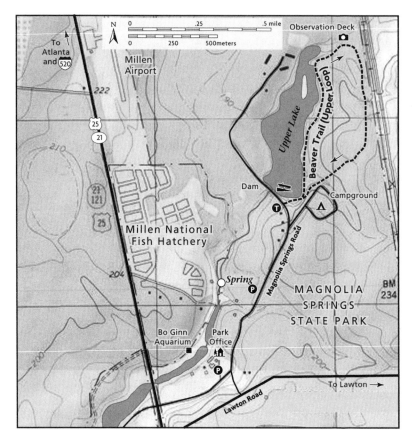

but Bo Ginn Aquarium is operated by the park and is a must-see during your visit here. The aquarium is open 9 AM to 4 PM daily and displays numerous native fish species.

The Beaver Trail (also known as the Upper Loop) is an easy hike that is great for smaller or older dogs that enjoy a brief trek into the forest. The short Beaver Trail loop starts near the boat dock, and the route closely follows the shoreline of Upper Lake, hiking in a clockwise direction. The terrain of Magnolia Springs State Park is typical of the coastal plains of Georgia, with fertile swamplands near the water, and sandy, dry ridges a short distance away. Wildlife is abundant, with various species of birds, reptiles (including alligators), and mammals inhabiting the area.

As the Beaver Trail reaches the northern end of the lake, look for a wooden observation deck. It offers an outstanding opportunity to take a break, see some wildlife, and look across the scenic Upper Lake. To prevent any unwelcome wildlife encounters, keep the dog on a leash here (as required by the park), then return to the trail as it begins looping around to the south. The Beaver Trail continues south through a drier and less dramatic section of trail as it curves for about 0.5 mile back to the trailhead where it started.

There are no backcountry campsites on the trail, but the 1071-acre Magnolia Spring State Park does have twenty-six tent, trailer, and RV campsites and three walk-in campsites that allow dogs.

20. Providence Canyon

Round trip: 7 miles
Difficulty: Easy to moderate
Hiking time: 3.5 hours
High point: 660 feet
Elevation gain: 280 feet
Best season: Spring, fall, winter
Maps: Providence Canyon State Park; USGS Lumpkin SW Quad
Contact: Providence Canyon State Park, Route One—Box 158, Lumpkin, GA 31815, (229) 838-6202, *www.gastateparks.org/info/providence*

Getting there: (From Atlanta, GA, 2.5 hours; from Lumpkin, GA, 20 minutes) Take US 27 from Columbus, GA, or US 27 north from Eufala, AL, to the town of Lumpkin. Turn west on Route 39C and drive 7 miles to the park. Follow the signs to the visitor center where trail maps and drinking water are available. The trail starts behind the main building.

The Providence Canyon area is known as "Georgia's Little Grand Canyon," for its unique geological features. The soils are very soft and erosive due to the elevation and geologic location of the park, and the area was

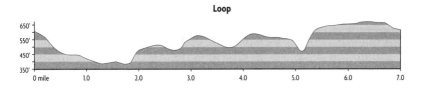

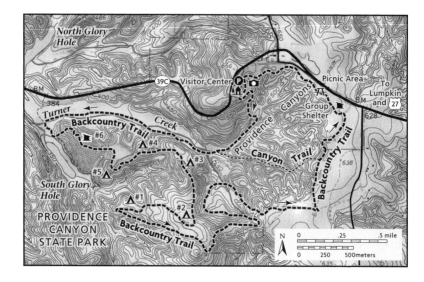

once an ancient seabed that was drastically affected by farming practices during the 1800s. Once trees and vegetation were removed, the soil eroded at an alarming rate. Ditches three to five feet deep were cut by the 1850s, and eventually the erosion led to sixteen canyons. Some are as deep as 150 feet and expose the colors of iron ore, manganese, kaolin, mica, and sandy clays.

There are two main canyon trails in the park. Day hikers can combine sections of the red-blazed Backcountry Trail with the white-blazed Canyon Trail for a 3-mile loop that runs around nine of the sixteen canyons. This hike is predominantly used by day hikers and would make an excellent outing for the novice hiker looking to spend some quality time outdoors with their dog. The descent into the canyon from the visitor center is of moderate grade and made up of several switchbacks. The ground on the rim of the canyons is dry, whereas the canyon floor is occasionally damp with water draining along the bottom of the sandy and moist ravine. The hike finishes with an ascent on the other side of the canyons and follows the rim back to the visitor center. The Canyon Trail offers several opportunities to view the beautiful, multi-layered colors of the canyon walls.

Our featured route is the red-blazed Backcountry Trail, which makes a 7-mile loop that circles the entire park and is used by both day hikers and overnight backpackers. The trail requires a permit to use any of the six campsites, all situated in a forested area. The trail offers views of the

Runaway erosion created "Georgia's Little Grand Canyon." This is a view of Providence Canyon looking north from the Backcountry Trail.

remaining seven canyons, which cannot be seen from the white-blazed Canyon Trail, so the longer route is well worth the effort if time is available.

From the visitor center, hike 0.75 mile on the white-blazed Canyon Trail once you reach the canyon floor. After leaving the main canyon, pick up the Backcountry Trail, which heads right (west) just after the Canyon Trail veers sharply left, and winds past each of the six campsites. Cross a wooden bridge, then begin a gradual climb to the first campsite #6 where there is a wood lean-to with a dirt floor in a small clearing.

From here, the trail winds by the remaining campsites—#5, #4, #3, #2, then #1—along the southern boundary of the park. All of the remaining sites are designed for tent camping, so no shelters are built in these areas. The trail continues past these tent sites until it turns north and meets up again with the Canyon Trail. Hikers and backpackers have the option of turning west and heading back to the visitor center; or can stay on the the red-blazed Backcountry Trail which follows the rim of the canyon, heading northwest past a group shelter, picnic area, and Route 39C back to the visitor center.

There are no drive-in campsites available at Providence Canyon State Park, but Florence Marina State Park is nearby and offers these services.

21. Oak Ridge Trail

Round trip: 2.6 miles
Difficulty: Easy
Hiking time: 1.5 hours
High point: 240 feet
Elevation gain: 81 feet
Best season: Any season
Map: USGS McRae Quad
Contact: Little Ocmulgee State Park, P.O. Box 97, McRae, GA 31055, (912) 868-2832

Getting there: (From Atlanta, GA, 3 hours; from Savannah, GA, 2 hours) In Atlanta, take I-75 south, then merge onto I-16 east, heading toward Savannah (Exit 165). Take Exit 51 (US 319) toward Dublin/McRae, and follow US 319 for 27 miles to the Little Ocmulgee State Park entrance, on the right. Follow the park entrance drive to the parking area next to the lodge and conference center, which is near the start of the trail.

Little Ocmulgee State Park in south Georgia offers a wide variety of recreational opportunities. There is the 18-hole Wallace Adams Golf Course, a 265-acre lake with boating, swimming, and fishing facilities, and for hikers, the Oak Ridge Trail. The park was once at the edge of an ancient ocean, so the terrain is composed of moist, fertile swamps with dry, sandy ridges—an interesting area to explore, for the day or over a weekend.

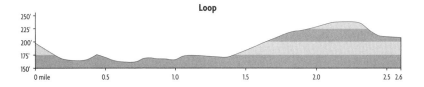

The 2.6-mile Oak Ridge Trail is a loop hike profiled here in a clockwise direction. To start the hike, leave the lodge and cross over a short boardwalk, heading southwest. Here the trail is typical of the coastal areas in eastern Georgia and South Carolina, with the moist, swampy terrain typical of the Low Country. Tupelo, cypress, maple, and longleaf pine are common trees in the area, and hikers might notice birds such as the blue heron soaring the skies around the dammed lake.

After crossing the boardwalk, the trail leads to a parking lot and then continues on past the group camping facility, headed northwest. As the loop hugs Little Ocmulgee Lake, it turns north with occasional views to the water. A cut-off trail (which makes a mini-loop) banks to the right as you near the north end of the lake. This forms the Magnolia Loop, which cuts some mileage off the hike and loops back to the starting point if you or the

Rebel contemplates a dip in a stream in North Georgia.

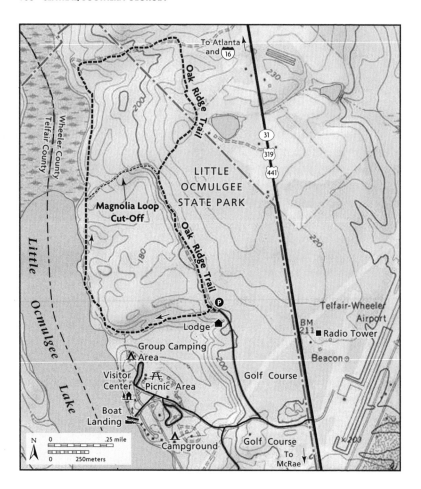

pooch need a shorter route. Otherwise, continue on for a short distance to a second boardwalk which leads to the water, with excellent views of Little Ocmulgee Lake and the marshy areas to the north. This is a great place to spot some of the numerous species of birds that frequent the park, and possibly take some photos. The dog might contemplate a dip in the water, but the park requires that dogs be leashed at all times. Sorry, pal.

The Oak Ridge Trail continues from the second boardwalk as it loops across the northern section of Little Ocmulgee Park and turns south back toward the trailhead. In this area, the terrain transitions from a swampy marshland to a dry and sandy coastal forest. The trees get less moisture in this area and are much smaller. Armadillo, gopher tortoise, and snakes are more prevalent since they like these drier and sandier conditions. Keep an eye out for these animals as you hike, but chances are that the pooch will spot them before you do.

While hiking south back toward the group camping area, the Magnolia Loop cut-off trail comes back in view on the right, then the Oak Ridge Trail eventually reaches the lodge where the hike started.

There are no backcountry campsites on this route, but Little Ocmulgee Park offers fifty-five campsites, the lodge, ten cabins, and a group campsite (near the trailhead). Dogs are not allowed in the lodge or in the cabins but can be in other areas of the park if leashed. Drinking water is available at the public source in the campground.

22. Gopher Loop Trail

Round trip: 1.5 miles
Difficulty: Easy
Hiking time: 1 hour
High point: 230 feet
Elevation gain: 55 feet
Best season: Spring, fall, winter
Maps: General Coffee State Park; USGS Douglas North Quad
Contact: General Coffee State Park, 46 John Coffee Road, Nicholls,
    GA 31554, (912) 384-7082

Getting there: (From Atlanta, GA, 4.5 hours; from Savannah, GA, 3 hours) On I-75, travel south to US 82 (Exit 62) in Tifton, then turn right and continue east. After 2.8 miles, take a slight left onto US 319 and continue for 18 miles. Go straight onto Route 32, and stay on Route 32 to the General Coffee State Park entrance, 6 miles east of Douglas, GA, on the left. The trailhead is located at Campground #1 about 1.5 miles down the main park road.

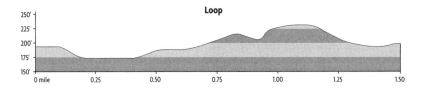

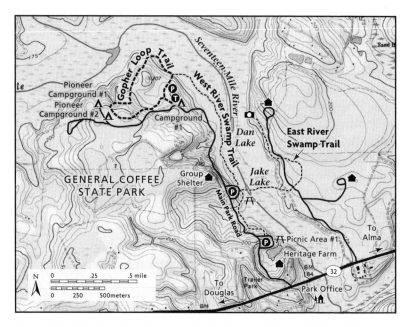

General Coffee State Park is named after General John Coffee, a U.S. congressman, military leader, and planter. The park is known for its rare and endangered species of plants and wildlife, mostly due to the interesting habitat formed in the park. The terrain changes considerably throughout the area, ranging from sandy ridges to moist, swampy lowlands. In addition to the wildlife, the park has a mock-farm that demonstrates early life in south Georgia. The Heritage Farm has log cabins, a corncrib, a tobacco barn, a cane mill, farm animals, and other exhibits.

A map of the state park is available at the visitor center. Drinking water is available from a public source in the park campground.

The Gopher Loop hike is one of three trails in this book within the boundaries of General Coffee State Park (see also Hikes 23 and 24). It begins in the northwestern corner of the park near Campground #1 and follows green blazes as it makes a 1.5-mile counterclockwise loop around a knob that sits at 207 feet overlooking the swamp surrounding Seventeen Mile River and Turkey Lake.

As the trail slowly turns to the northwest, it follows along the edge of an ancient region that is part of the park's Sandhill Management Area. The longleaf–turkey oak sandhill ecosystem is the most highly endangered ecosystem in the Southeast, and is home to many threatened and protected species of plants and animals. Your dog may notice the numerous

Rebel scratches his back after setting up our campsite for the night.

gopher tortoise burrows while walking the trail, so keep the leash tight so these protected animals and their homes are not destroyed. The burrows may extend up to 30 feet underground and be up to 6 feet below the surface level, and are home not only to the gopher tortoise but also to over 100 other species of other animals.

As the Gopher Loop Trail turns to the southwest, passes near the Pioneer Campgrounds, and makes the final turn east back to the trailhead, keep an eye out for some of the many species of snakes that are found in General Coffee State Park, including the endangered indigo snake and several types of rattlesnakes. The sound of a rattlesnake is sure to make any hiker or canine anxious, so stay on the trail and keep a safe distance from any snake—especially a poisonous one.

For those who wish to make this an overnight adventure, there are fifty campsites and six cottages in the park. In addition, the Burnham House, an elegantly decorated nineteenth-century cabin with hand-stitched quilts and Persian rugs, is another option. Dogs are not allowed in the majority of the cottages but are allowed in other areas of the park as long as they are on a leash no longer than six feet. Recently, a single dog-friendly cottage was made available to the public for an extra fee (on top of the normal cottage rates).

23. West River Swamp Trail

Round trip: 2.8 miles
Difficulty: Easy
Hiking time: 1–2 hours
High point: 175 feet
Elevation gain: Negligible
Best season: Spring, fall, winter
Map: USGS McRae Quad
Contact: General Coffee State Park, 46 John Coffee Road, Nicholls, GA 31554, (912) 384-7082

Getting there: (From Atlanta, GA, 4.5 hours; from Savannah, GA, 3 hours) On I-75, travel south to US 82 (Exit 62) in Tifton. Turn right and continue east. After 2.8 miles, take a slight left onto US 319 and continue for 18 miles. Remain traveling straight to go onto Route 32. The entrance to General Coffee State Park is 6 miles east of Douglas, GA, on Route 32, on the left. The trailhead is 0.5 mile into the park off Route 32, on the right.

The West River Swamp Trail is one of three trails in this book within the boundaries of General Coffee State Park. (For more information about the park, see Gopher Loop Trail, Hike 22.) This hike begins in the southern portion of General Coffee State Park, just past the Heritage Farm at Picnic Area 1. The trail follows blue blazes northbound on a 1.4-mile in-and-out route along the Seventeen Mile River, heading northwest past Dan and Jake Lakes.

Although the lakes sound inviting, dogs must be kept on a leash at all times. This is for their protection since the swamp has numerous poisonous snakes (including the water moccasin or cottonmouth, native to this area). The park is no place for the pooch to be wandering aimlessly.

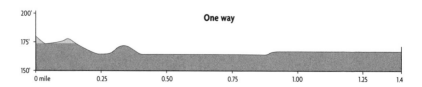

Before heading out on the trail, pick up a park map at the visitor center. Drinking water is available from a public source in the park campground.

The start of the trail winds through an area of longleaf pine and mixed hardwoods and down to the edge of the river. As the trail meets the Seventeen Mile River, it turns northwest to follow along the edge of the river. This section of the trail is close to the river edge and may flood during times of high water. Watch out for exposed roots and stumps in this section of the trail.

After approximately 0.5 mile along this route, the boardwalk and the beginning of the East River Swamp Trail appear on the right with a parking area on the left. Continue ahead, and walk along the Seventeen Mile River to the end of the West River Swamp Trail at the Gopher Loop. Birds frequent the swampy marshland along the river, and the trail is a great place to spot wildlife to the east. During the summer months, carry insect repellent, particularly in the morning or evening hours, and consider products like Frontline and Advantix which contain flea, tick, and insect repellent for dogs. DEET-based solutions are not recommended for your pet.

The end of the trail winds through an area of longleaf pine and mixed hardwoods down to the edge of the river where it meets with the Gopher

Rebel circles back on the trail to greet backpackers Steve Snyder, Joe Fess, and Glenn Schuffenhauer.

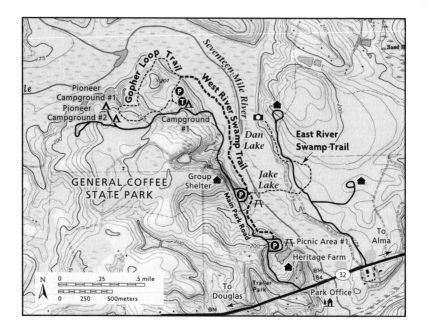

Loop. This section of the trail is close to the river edge and may flood during times of high water, so watch out for exposed roots and stumps. From here you have the option of backtracking to the trailhead or adding 1.2 miles to your hike by completing the Gopher Loop.

For those wishing to make this an overnight adventure, there are fifty campsites and six cottages in the park. (See Hike 22 for more information on accommodations and dog policies in the park.)

24. East River Swamp Trail

Round trip: 1.5 miles

Difficulty: Easy

Hiking time: 1 hour

High point: 187 feet

Elevation gain: Negligible

Best season: Spring, fall, winter

Maps: General Coffee State Park; USGS Douglas North Quad

Contact: General Coffee State Park, 46 John Coffee Road, Nicholls, GA 31554, (912) 384-7082

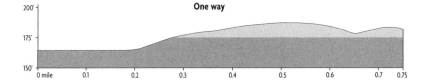

Getting there: (From Atlanta, GA, 4.5 hours; from Savannah, GA, 3 hours) On I-75, travel south to US 82 (Exit 62) in Tifton, then turn right and continue east. After 2.8 miles, take a slight left onto US 319 and continue for 18 miles. Go straight onto Route 32, and stay on Route 32 to the General Coffee State Park entrance, 6 miles east of Douglas, GA, on the left. The trailhead is about 0.8 mile into the park, just past the parking area for the West River Swamp Trail (Hike 23).

The East River Swamp Trail, one of three trails featured in General Coffee State Park, begins near Picnic Area #1 south of Jake Lake. (For more information about the park, see the Gopher Loop Trail, Hike 22.) The in-and-out hike, blazed in pink, heads east across the Seventeen Mile River over an elevated boardwalk that allows hikers and their dogs an opportunity to experience the river ecosystem without getting the paws wet. Wading

Katie (a golden retriever) enjoys some leftovers after a backcountry meal on the trail.

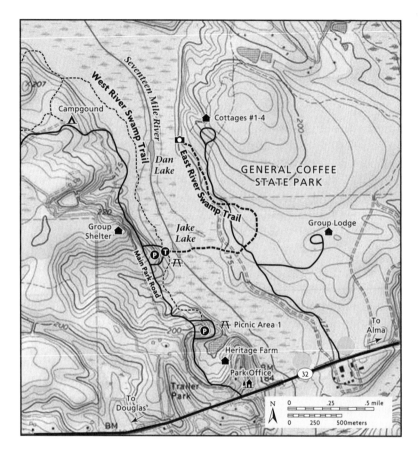

birds and river otters visit the swamp during the wet season, so keep an eye out for wildlife while you cross the river. Hikers who visit during a dry spring and summer may not see the river, as it can completely dry up during periods of infrequent rain. (Drinking water is available from a public source in the park campground.)

The trail continues past the boardwalk, then winds over and back across a park road that leads to cottages #1 to #4 as it turns back to the northwest. It ends past a small sandhill area at a large southern magnolia tree behind the rental cottages just east of Dan Lake. Hikers must backtrack to the trailhead on the return trip, which can be made either on the trail or partly by paved road. For those who wish to make this an overnight adventure, there are fifty campsites and six cottages in the park. (See Hike 22 for more information on accommodations and dog policies in the park.)

PART 3

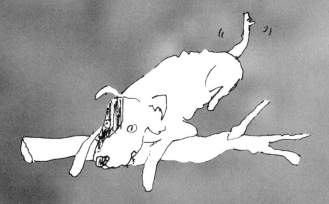

South Carolina

Northwestern South Carolina

25. Ellicott Rock

Round trip: 7.0 miles
Difficulty: Easy to moderate
Hiking time: 3–4 hours
High point: 2350 feet
Elevation gain: 300 feet
Best season: Spring, fall, winter
Maps: Chattooga National Wild and Scenic River; USGS Cashiers Quad
Contact: Sumter National Forest, Andrew Pickens Ranger District,
112 Andrew Pickens Circle, Mountain Rest, SC 29664,
(864) 638-9568, *www.fs.fed.us/r8/fms*

Getting there: (From Greenville, SC, 1 hour; from Clayton, GA, 45 minutes) At US 76 and US 441 in Clayton, GA, take a right onto Rickman Road and continue for 0.5 mile. Turn right onto Warwoman Road and head 14 miles to Route 28. Take a right onto Route 28 and follow it for 1.8 miles to Forest Road 646 (also known as Burrells Ford Road). Follow FR 646 (mostly a gravel road) for about 9 miles to a wooden bridge that crosses

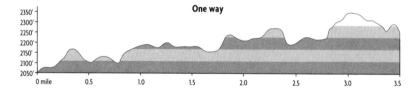

One way

the Chattooga River. The trailhead is immediately ahead on the left and many people park on the side of the road in this area. Another option is to continue on for about half a mile to the Burrell Ford Parking Area, which is a designated US Forest Service parking lot. Please note that Forest Road 646 becomes Forest Road 708 when you cross the bridge over the Chattooga River and enter South Carolina.

Andrew Ellicott, a noted surveyor, was commissioned by North Carolina and Georgia to determine the boundary between the states. He completed his survey in 1811 by chiseling an inconspicuous mark on a rock on the east bank of the Chattooga River. This rock, at the 35th parallel, is found inside the Ellicott Rock Wilderness of the Sumter National Forest and is named Ellicott Rock after its founder.

There are actually two rocks that mark the boundary between the states. Two years after Ellicott's efforts, a commission was created to establish the border of North Carolina and South Carolina at the 35th parallel. This boundary mark was chiseled into a rock, known as Commissioners Rock, which often fools hikers into thinking it is actually Ellicott Rock.

The Chattooga River Trail to Ellicott Rock, marked with black double blazes, is located on the forest road about 0.5 mile from the Burrells Ford parking area. If approached from 646 in Georgia, it is on the left just after the wooden bridge over the Chattooga River.

Congress designated the Chattooga as a Wild and Scenic River on May 10, 1974, and the river is one of a few remaining free-flow streams in the Southeast, flowing south for 10 miles to North Carolina and for 40 miles as the state boundary between South Carolina and Georgia.

The trail follows the Chattooga River for the entire hike to Ellicott Rock, and there are plenty of opportunities for a swim here. Your trail hound will most certainly love this hike if he enjoys water.

Start at the trail sign just off FR 708. After about 0.3 mile, the Chattooga River Trail intersects with the Spoonauger Falls Trail and it is well worth the side hike to this beautiful waterfall. Watch the side trail carefully, however, since it switches back over a small hill to reach the falls after only a few hundred feet. Spoonauger Falls makes an excellent photo opportunity.

Once you backtrack to the Chattooga River Trail, continue northeast, to the 0.7-mile mark where the white-blazed Foothills Trail enters from the right (it is 1.6 miles on the Foothills Trail to the Burrells Ford parking

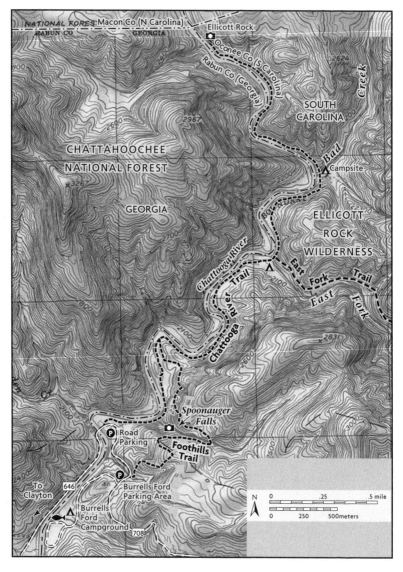

area if you prefer to park there). Continue ahead following the black blazes along the Chattooga River rolling up and down with some slight elevation change until the trail reaches the East Fork of the Chattooga River about 1.8 miles from the trailhead. Here are some flat areas for camping and an 80-foot bridge over the East Fork of the Chattooga River. Running along the East Fork (which looks more like a stream) is the East Fork Trail, which leads uphill to the right for 2.5 miles to the Walhalla

Fish Hatchery. Parking and a picnic area are also nearby and are used by hikers and backpackers to reach Ellicott Rock. Pass the East Fork Trail and continue along the Chattooga River Trail heading north. At the 2.4-mile mark, a wide-open flat area is visible at Bad Creek, which offers another opportunity for overnight camping. The campsite sits in a densely wooded area that is suitable for a large group, with opportunities for trout fishing nearby on the river. The U.S. Forest Service recommends catch-and-release fishing in this area, and if you catch a trout with a tag, please let them know by completing a form available from a small metal box along the main trail.

To reach Ellicott Rock, continue hiking 1.1 mile past Bad Creek along the Chattooga River until reaching another short wooden foot bridge. At this point, begin to look for Ellicott Rock and Commissioners Rock. There is a tree above the river's edge with a small metal disc nailed to it. Backtrack approximately 25 feet to an embankment and climb down to the Chattooga River. Here you'll find "LAT 35, AD 1813, NC+SC" carved into Commissioners Rock. The spot is sometimes marked with a red or

Roger Cardoe and Rebel hike on the Chattooga River Trail, near Ellicott Rock.

pink streamer, but the rock may be obscured during times of high water when it sits below the surface of the river.

To find Ellicott Rock, look upstream 15 feet. This stone is three to four feet higher than Commissioners Rock and farther from the edge of the water. All that can be seen in this rock is "NC."

For those who decide to make this an overnight adventure, there are numerous wilderness campsites along the river, at the East Fork, and at Bad Creek. Another option is to use the facilities at Burrells Ford Campground, which requires a short hike from the Burrells Ford parking area. Although it is heavily used, particularly on weekends, the Burrells Ford Campground has a number of sites, and it is convenient to the parking area, which has a pit toilet. Keep in mind that the national forest requires that you camp at least 50 feet from the river.

City slickers may prefer to camp in the nearby Oconee State Park, which has nineteen cabins (each able to sleep four to eight people), 140 campsites, and ten tent sites. Pets are not allowed in the cabins or in the cabin areas but are permitted in most of the outdoor areas. Check *www. southcarolinaparks.com* for current rates and restrictions. Pets must also be on a leash no longer than six feet in length.

26. King Creek Falls

Round trip: 2 miles
Difficulty: Easy to moderate
Hiking time: 1 hour
High point: 2225 feet
Elevation gain: 80 feet
Best season: Any season
Maps: Chattooga National Wild and Scenic River; USGS
  Tamassee Quad
Contact: Sumter National Forest, Andrew Pickens Ranger District,
  112 Andrew Pickens Circle, Mountain Rest, SC 29664,
  (864) 638-9568, *www.fs.fed.us/r8/fms*

Getting there: (From Greenville, SC, 1 hour; from Clayton, GA, 45 minutes) At US 76 and 441 in Clayton, GA, take a right onto Rickman Road and continue for 0.5 mile. Turn right onto Warwoman Road and continue 14 miles. Take a right onto Route 28 and follow it for 1.8 miles

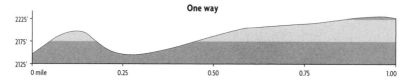

to Forest Road 646 (also known as Burrells Ford Road). Follow Forest Road 646 for 9.4 miles to the Burrells Ford parking area. Forest Road 646 will become gravel for a majority of the drive. In South Carolina, this road becomes Forest Road 708.

This is one of three featured hikes along the Chattooga River (see also Hikes 25 and 28). Designated a Wild and Scenic River, the Chattooga is one of the few remaining free-flow streams in the Southeast. Be sure to bring a map from home; there is no good place to get one near the river.

The hike to King Creek Falls is an easy one that follows the river via black double blazes, heading southbound from the Burrells Ford parking area. After about 0.3 mile, you'll pick up a spur trail that leads through a dense forest of hardwoods to the waterfall. Here King Creek drops 60 to 70 feet into a U-shaped cove that has a small beach and a nice swimming hole at the base of the falls. This is a spectacular site, and both you and your dog are likely to enjoy splashing around in the pool—particularly on a hot summer day.

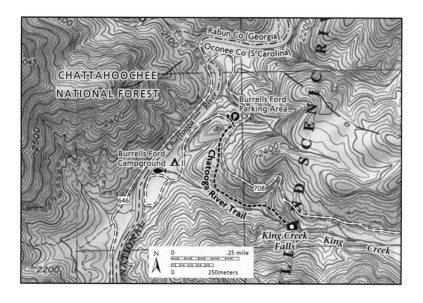

Enjoying the cool waters of the Chattooga River after a hot day of backpacking

For those looking for an overnight adventure, there are a couple of camping options in the area. One is to use the facilities at Burrells Ford Campground (a short walk from the Burrells Ford parking area); for more information, see Hike 25. Burrells Ford is heavily used, particularly on weekends, but it has designated sites with picnic tables and fire rings, and is located right near the Chattooga River.

Another overnight option is to wilderness camp along the Chattooga River. No backcountry camping is allowed within 50 feet of the river, but there are numerous campsites in both directions along the water, and no permit is required. Although this backtrack hike is fairly easy, it gets considerably more challenging as the trail winds its way south along the Chattooga River. Overnight backpackers should keep this in mind when hiking southbound along the Chattooga River from King Creek Falls.

27. Long Mountain

Distance: 8 miles one way (shuttle hike)
Difficulty: Moderate
Hiking time: 4–5 hours
High point: 2300 feet
Elevation gain: 800 feet
Best season: Any season
Maps: USGS Tamassee and Walhalla Quads
Contact: Sumter National Forest, Andrew Pickens Ranger District, 112 Andrew Pickens Circle, Mountain Rest, SC, 29664, (864) 638-9568; Oconee State Park, 624 State Park Road, Mountain Rest, SC 29664, (864) 638-5353

Getting there: (From Greenville, SC, 1.5 hours; from Atlanta, GA, 2.5 hours) At I-85 on Lake Hartwell, take Exit 1 and follow Route 11 toward Walhalla. At the junction of Routes 11 and 28, take Route 28 through Walhalla and continue for approximately 10 miles. At the junction with Route 107, turn right onto Route 107. After 2 miles, you'll reach the entrance to Oconee State Park. A car can be left here, at the southern terminus of this hike. To reach the north trailhead where this hike begins, continue on Route 107 for an additional 3.7 miles to Forest Road 710. Go about 500 yards, and the designated parking area is on the right.

Oconee State Park is an 1165-acre park located near Mountain Rest, South Carolina, with recreational opportunities that include hiking, camping, fishing, and boating. The park is bordered by Sumter National Forest and is the trailhead for the 85-mile Foothills Trail. The trail crosses some of the most rugged and beautiful terrain in the Southeast, and provides access to major mountain streams and breathtaking views including Sassafras Mountain, the highest peak in South Carolina. This hike is on the final

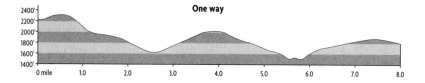

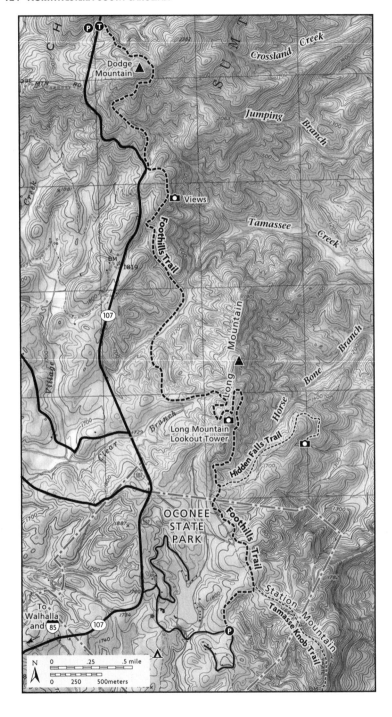

Socked in with fog at the trailhead

two sections of this well-maintained footpath (listed as sections A12 through A14 in the *Foothills Trail Guide*) and it finishes at the western terminus of the route, located within the Oconee State Park boundary.

The one-way, shuttle hike over Long Mountain begins at a small parking area just off Route 107 on Forest Road 710. The route includes a side trip to Hidden Falls, which adds 2 miles to the route. (Hikers also have the option of skipping the side hike and cutting the mileage down to 6.0 miles.)

To start the route, park a car at both ends of the trail, then ascend briefly from Route 107 for about 0.5 mile around the eastern side of Dodge Mountain. There are some decent views in this area looking down at the valley to the east.

From Dodge Mountain, begin a gradual descent over the next 2 miles and intersect with Route 107 again on the right. There is a parking area here as well, but continue over a series of two small streams with wooden bridges to stay on the white-blazed trail. The pooch may enjoy a quick drink here, especially on a hot summer day. Fortunately, this section is not heavily traveled, and you might have some leeway with the leash.

After 4 miles, there is a spur trail to the fire tower on Long Mountain. This is a great place to take a break and mark the halfway point in the hike. There are spectacular views of the Piedmont from Long Mountain, particularly in the winter months. It's nearly a 600-foot climb to the summit, so relax and let the hound enjoy the moment.

From Long Mountain, the trail descends again over the next 2 miles and eventually enters Oconee State Park. Leash laws are enforced here, so make sure the pooch is attached when the boundary between Sumter National Forest and the state park is crossed. There is a yellow-blazed side trail on the left to Hidden Falls just before you reach the park border. The Hidden Falls Trail leads to a 50-foot cascade, well worth the 2-mile side trip if time permits. Use caution when walking on the slippery rock at the base of the falls, however, since an ankle (or paw) gets twisted on occasion at this site.

The final 2 miles of trail ascend gradually to Oconee State Park where the Foothills Trail completes its 85-mile journey. Make sure to stay with the white blazes of the Foothills Trail to finish in the correct parking area at Oconee State Park. Just 0.4 mile from the end of the route, the red-blazed Tamassee Knob Trail breaks off to the left.

For those who would like to make this an overnight adventure, there are 150 campground sites (including ten walk-in campsites) and nineteen cabins (no dogs permitted) in Oconee State Park. Backpackers can also camp on the Foothills Trail in the Sumter National Forest section of the Foothills Trail. Check with the Forest Service for more information.

28. Lick Log Creek Falls

Round trip: 9 miles
Difficulty: Easy to moderate
Hiking time: 4 hours
High point: 1725 feet
Elevation gain: 125 feet
Best season: Any season
Maps: Chattooga National Wild and Scenic River; USGS Satolah Quad
Contact: Sumter National Forest, Andrew Pickens Ranger District,
    112 Andrew Pickens Circle, Mountain Rest, SC 29664,
    (864) 638-9568, *www.fs.fed.us/r8/fms*

Getting there: (From Atlanta, GA, 2.5 hours; from Walhalla, SC, 15 minutes) At the junction of Routes 28 and 107 8 miles north of Walhalla, SC,

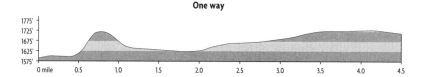

take Route 28 north and follow it across the Chattooga River into Georgia. Continue 8.6 miles to a gravel road, Forest Road 784. Parking is available on this road in an undesignated lot. This lot is more primitive, yet closer to the trailhead. A designated parking lot (the Russell Bridge parking area) is also available 0.2 mile north on Route 28, across the river.

This is one of three featured hikes along the Chattooga River (see also Hikes 25 and 26). Designated a Wild and Scenic River, the Chattooga is one of the few remaining free-flow streams in the Southeast. Don't forget a map as none are available in the area.

The trail to Lick Log Creek Falls is an in-and-out hike that begins at Russell Bridge along Route 28 and follows the banks of the Chattooga River for roughly 4.5 miles. Watch the route carefully as you leave the parking area, however, since the trail begins by veering to the right and makes a mild 200-foot climb over a small ridge in the process. It is easier and more tempting to keep walking straight on a side path beaten down by trout fishermen, but this route is a dead-end that stops abruptly at the water's edge. Instead, follow the black double blazes of the Chattooga River Trail as it loops around Brack Hill, which can be seen across the water.

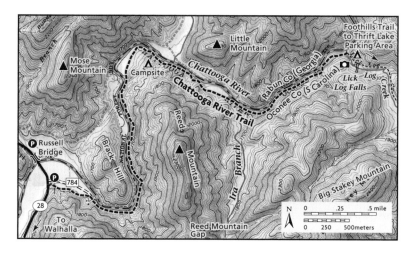

Lick Log Creek Falls as seen from the Chattooga River Trail

At this point, the route turns north and descends along Reed Mountain back to the Chattooga River at 1600 feet. At mile 1.3, the trail merges with an old road and continues through a hardwood forest. There are nice campsites situated along the river on the northernmost edge of Reed Mountain. Here the trail turns to the southeast and generally hugs the banks of the Chattooga for the next few miles.

At mile 3.4, there is a wooden bridge over Ira Branch, and Lick Log Creek Falls is about a mile away. Cross the stream, and continue along the Chattooga River to Lick Log Creek at mile 4.0. Here the Chattooga River Trail breaks away from the river and follows Lick Log Creek about 0.5 mile to a small pool and 20-foot waterfall. Your dog will enjoy frolicking in the pool, especially after a tough day of hiking.

Continue across a small bridge just before you reach the pool and waterfall at mile 4.5. This is an excellent place to take a break and enjoy the scenery. The falls form a two-tiered drop, and there are flat areas for camping nearby for overnight backpackers. It is worth noting that hikers and backpackers can also access this Lick Log Creek Falls from the Thrift Lake area, roughly 2 miles away—so the Reed Mountain campsites along the Chattooga may provide more privacy for overnight backpackers.

29. Yellow Branch Falls

Round trip: 3 miles
Difficulty: Easy to moderate
Hiking time: 1–2 hours
High point: 1540 feet
Elevation gain: 370 feet
Best season: Any season
Maps: Sumter National Forest; USGS Whetstone Quad
Contact: Sumter National Forest, Andrew Pickens Ranger District, 112 Andrew Pickens Circle, Mountain Rest, SC 29664, (864) 638-9568, *www.fs.fed.us/r8/fms*; Oconee State Park, (864) 638-5353

Getting there: (From Atlanta, GA, 2.5 hours; from Walhalla, SC, 15 minutes) From Walhalla, drive west on Route 28 for 6.8 miles and turn left into the Yellow Branch picnic ground.

Located in the northwest corner of South Carolina, Sumter National Forest is comprised of three ranger districts, including the 79,000-acre Andrew Pickens Ranger District, which forms the western boundary of the Chattooga River (see Hikes 25, 26, and 28). This in-and-out hike to Yellow Branch Falls is located within the Andrew Pickens Ranger District and travels over moderate terrain to end at a beautiful, cascading waterfall with numerous rivulets that drop roughly 50 feet. The National Forest Service recommends that you wear sturdy shoes and use extra caution during wet conditions on this hike, since the trail skirts the edges of deep ravines.

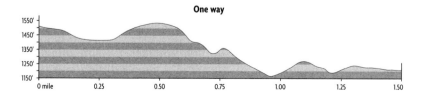

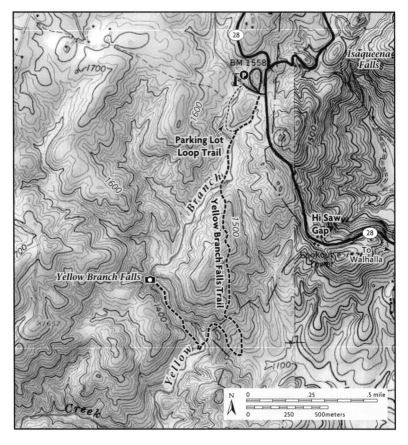

The hike begins at the picnic area off Route 28 and follows a connector trail for 0.2 mile. From here, the path makes a sharp turn to join the Yellow Branch Falls Trail for approximately 1.3 miles. It then descends to a spectacular view and pool at the base of the waterfalls. This is a great place to wade in the stream with your dog and enjoy a refreshing dip before heading back to the trailhead. It is particularly invigorating during the hot and humid months that are common to this area in the summer.

During the hike, the trail passes through groves of dignified hardwoods and meanders across a number of small streams. This makes for an excellent hike any time of the year. In the winter months, look south to see the small community of Walhalla in the distance.

The easy terrain and attractive scenery have made the trail quite popular, particularly on weekends. It may be helpful to take a leash up to six feet long, although it is not required in the national forest. Unfortunately,

Yellow Branch Falls as seen from the terminus of the hiking trail

there are no decent spots for camping near the base of the falls, and the only flat areas are close to the trailhead.

The best option for camping near Yellow Branch Falls is at Oconee State Park (see also Hike 27), which is approximately 10 miles away and has nineteen cabins (each able to sleep four to eight people), 140 campsites, and ten tent sites. Pets are not allowed in the cabins or in the cabin areas but are permitted in most of the outdoor areas. For current rates and restrictions, check *www.southcarolinaparks.com*. Pets must also be on a leash no longer than six feet in length. Additional recreational activities at the park include fishing, swimming, and boating in two small lakes.

30. Matthews Creek

Round trip: 8.6 miles
Difficulty: Easy to moderate
Hiking time: 4.5 hours
High point: 3173 feet
Elevation gain: 1473 feet
Best season: Any season
Maps: Mountain Bridge Wilderness and Recreation Area; USGS
Table Rock Quad
Contact: Caesars Head State Park, 8155 Greer Highway, Cleveland,
SC 29635, (864) 836-6115; Table Rock State Park, (864) 878-9813

Getting there: (From Atlanta, GA, 3 hours; from Marietta, SC, 35 minutes) In Greenville, SC, take US 276 north approximately 25 miles to Caesars Head State Park. There is a visitor center and parking area on the left. From here, drive north on US 276 for about 1.1 miles to the Raven Cliff Falls parking area on the right side on the road. Walk across US 276 to the trailhead for Raven Cliff Falls, on the south side of the road. (There is another trailhead in the parking lot that leads to a different destination.)

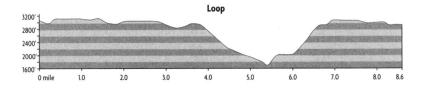

The hike to Matthews Creek is one of three featured hikes in the 10,000-acre Mountain Bridge Wilderness Area, which includes 7467 acres of Caesars Head State Park and Jones Gap State Park (see also Hikes 31 and 32). This loop hike in Caesars Head State Park can be done in either direction, but a counterclockwise hike is profiled here. It begins at the trailhead off US 276, 1.1 miles north of the visitor center at Caesars Head State Park.

The blue-blazed Gum Gap Trail shares the first 1.4 miles of the route with the red-blazed Raven Cliff Falls Trail (see Hike 32). The path heads west through a forest of hardwoods, where there is very little elevation change over the first few miles.

When the blue and red blazes split at the 1.4 mile mark, turn right and follow the blue-blazed Gum Gap Trail for another 1.5 miles until it meets the pink-blazed Naturaland Trust Trail.

At this point, the blue blazes leave the state park boundary and follow the Foothills Trail. There is a nice campsite just ahead on the left side of the trail, just over 3 miles from the trailhead, if you plan to make this an overnight backcountry trip.

Otherwise, begin a gradual descent along the Naturaland Trust Trail to the Raven Cliff Falls suspension bridge, which is positioned a short distance from the top of the 400-foot waterfall. Although the bridge offers fantastic views of Matthews Creek and the surrounding valley, Raven Cliff Falls cannot be seen from the bridge—but can from an excellent

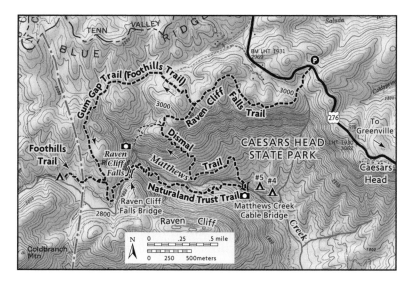

Roger Cardoe and Chris Kasischke cross the cable bridge over Matthews Creek, which drops to form Raven Cliff Falls.

viewpoint on a side trail farther around the loop. For access to the viewing platform, cross the suspension bridge and begin a long, steep descent with numerous switchbacks that eventually lead to Matthews Creek and a set of two cables that hang over the river.

At this point, you have two options. You can either work your way across the cables (and above the river), or you can wade across the occasionally knee-deep water. Whatever you decide, make sure to unbuckle your hip belt if you are carrying a backpack, and remove your dog's pack if she is carrying one as well. If either of you lose your balance, you do not want the backpack to drag you to the bottom of the river.

Matthews Creek is a great place to take a break or even to book a backcountry campsite. You are also likely to enjoy the challenging but entertaining cable crossing of the river. The climb back to the trailhead is not easy, however. So both owner and pet should load up on water and cool off in the creek before making the climb out of the ravine.

The purple-blazed Dismal Trail is just across Matthews Creek and leads 1.5 miles up a steep slope to reconnect with the red-blazed Raven Cliff Falls Trail. For outstanding views of the waterfall, turn left and hike the 0.3 mile southwest down to the wooden observation deck of Raven Cliff Falls, likely to be the highlight of your trip.

From the falls, backtrack to rejoin the loop, as you gradually ascend back to 3000 feet via the Raven Cliff Falls Trail. About 0.6 mile beyond the observation platform, the Raven Cliff Falls Trail rejoins the blue-blazed Gum Gap Trail, and the two trails wind their way back to the parking area.

If you choose to make this an overnight experience, there are numerous campsites along Matthews Creek in Caesars Head State Park—twenty-four primitive campsites, and eighteen that provide fire pits. Group sites can be reserved for ten to twenty people. Each site requires a backcountry permit. Backpackers should check with the visitor center for availability before heading out on their overnight adventure. Fires are only permitted in designated fire pits, so make sure to take a backcountry stove and practice leave-no-trace guidelines since Matthews Creek is your water source for these backcountry campsites.

City slickers may opt for an in-and-out day hike to Raven Cliff Falls (see Hike 32) and head to the nearby Table Rock State Park, which has cabins and a campground. The park provides a sixty-nine-site camping area, located near the park entrance, and a twenty-five-site camping area, located near White Oaks picnic area. Three primitive areas with central water and privy are available for organized groups. Table Rock State Park also has some rustic cabins which are completely furnished, heated, air-conditioned, and supplied with bath and bed linens, basic cooking and eating utensils, automatic coffee maker, a microwave, and include a screened porch and fireplace. Pets are not allowed in the cabins or in the cabin areas but are permitted in most of the outdoor areas. Check *www.southcarolinaparks.com* for current rates and restrictions. Pets must also be on a leash no longer than six feet in length.

31. Middle Saluda River

Distance: 5.3 miles one way (shuttle hike)
Difficulty: Easy to moderate
Hiking time: 3 hours
High point: 3300 feet
Elevation gain: 1900 feet
Best season: Spring, fall, winter
Maps: Mountain Bridge Wilderness Area; USGS Cleveland Quad
Contact: Jones Gap State Park, 303 Jones Gap Road, Marietta, SC
29661, (864) 836-3647, *www.discoversouthcarolina.com/stateparks/
parklocator.asp*

Getting there: (From Atlanta, GA, 3 hours; from Marietta, SC, 35 minutes) To reach Jones Gap State Park, the eastern trailhead for this shuttle hike, follow US 276 north from Greenville, SC for 20 miles to Cleveland, SC. Jones Gap State Park is located just west of Cleveland, SC on US 276 north. A shuttle vehicle should be left here since the western trailhead is located in Caesars Head State Park, which is 15 miles to the west. To reach Caesars Head, continue on US 276 north and drive up a steep hill to the visitors center near the top of the mountain and on the left. Trail maps are available inside. The western trailhead is at the Raven Cliff Falls parking area 1.1 miles north on US 276 and located on your right.

The 3346-acre Jones Gap State Park is located in the 10,000-acre Mountain Bridge Wilderness Area. The park encompasses the Middle Saluda River, designated as South Carolina's first scenic river. More than 400 species of flora, including rare and endangered plants, and state record trees are found in the park. The Environmental Education Center offers nature exhibits and a lab area to explore. Portions of the old Cleveland Fish Hatchery have been restored and are stocked with trout (for observation

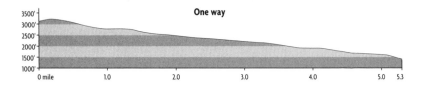

only), and the park has over 50 miles of hiking trails and is also an access point to the Foothills Hiking Trail via the Jones Gap Trail.

Solomon Jones built the Jones Gap Trail as a toll road in the 1800s, and it was used for this purpose until about 1910. What is now US 276 became the route used by motorists.

This shuttle hike begins at the Raven Cliff Falls parking lot (where the toll road crossed the ridge) and travels east, culminating at the Jones Gap State Park trailhead. The hike leaves the lot following the Tom Miller Trail, and after 0.8 mile intersects with the blue-blazed Jones Gap Trail. Here the route turns right and follows the Jones Gap Trail another 4.5 miles to

Daisy explores a pool along the Middle Saluda River.

the Jones Gap State Park parking lot, following the Middle Saluda River almost the entire route.

The hike crosses the river several times, making this route a favorite for dogs who enjoy the water. Along the hike, there are also several small but scenic waterfalls tucked along the Middle Saluda River. One in particular drops about 15 feet after about 3.5 miles, and there is a nice wading pool at its base.

For those looking for an overnight adventure, there are several campsites along the trail at various distances from either trailhead. Eighteen designated sites are situated along the Jones Gap Trail and each is close to the Middle Saluda River. The state park has designated two of these sites for large groups, but all require a backcountry permit. So check with the Caesars Head or Jones Gap State Park office for reservations and for more information on fees, regulations, and availability before heading out. The river is the water source for all of these campsites, but nearby Table Rock State Park has drive-in campsites for those who prefer flush toilets, picnic tables, and park amenities to backcountry camping.

32. Raven Cliff Falls

Round trip: 4 miles
Difficulty: Moderate
Hiking time: 2 hours
High point: 3173 feet
Elevation gain: 673 feet
Best season: Any season
Maps: Mountain Bridge Wilderness and Recreation Area; USGS Table Rock Quad
Contact: Caesars Head State Park, 8155 Geer Highway, Cleveland, SC 29635, (864) 836-6115, *www.discoversouthcarolina.com/stateparks/parklocator.asp*

Getting there: (From Atlanta, GA, 3 hours; from Marietta, SC, 35 minutes) In Greenville, SC, take US 276 north approximately 25 miles to Caesars Head State Park. There is a visitor center and parking area on the left where you can pick up a trail map. From here, drive north on US 276 for about 1.1 miles to the Raven Cliff Falls parking area on the right side of the road. Walk across US 276 to the trailhead for Raven Cliff Falls, on the

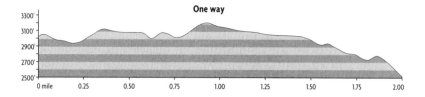

south side of the road. (There is another trailhead in the parking lot that leads to a different destination.)

Raven Cliff Falls is one of three featured hikes in the 10,000-acre Mountain Bridge Wilderness Area, which includes Caesars Head State Park along with Jones Gap State Park (see also Hikes 30 and 31).

This in-and-out hike follows the Raven Cliff Falls Trail, an old buggy road marked by red blazes that shares the first 1.4 miles with the blue-blazed Gum Gap Trail. Due to the beauty of the waterfall and the popularity of Caesars Head State Park, the trail is heavily traveled on weekends, and the two-lane US 276 normally has a steady stream of traffic on it. Make sure to leash your dog at the parking area and not at the trailhead, since it is necessary to cross the street to start the hike.

Leaving the trailhead, follow the red and blue blazes, heading west through a forest of hardwoods. There is very little elevation change over the first 1.5 miles, which makes this a pleasant walk through a mature Southern forest. You and the pooch will enjoy this easy section of trail.

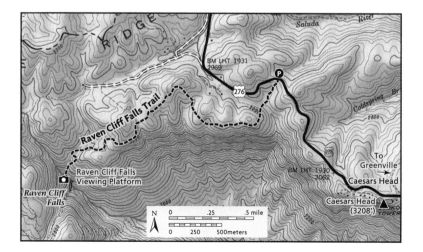

At the 1.4-mile mark, the blue-blazed Gum Gap Trail forks right and the red blazed Raven Cliff Falls Trail turns left. Follow the red blazes and begin a gradual descent heading southwest. The trail becomes steeper as hikers close in on the wooden observation platform, but the views of Raven Cliff Falls are outstanding and make the hike well worth the effort. The falls drop roughly 400 feet before pouring into Matthews Creek and heading southeast through Caesars Head State Park.

The 420-foot Raven Cliff Falls as seen from the viewing platform

For those who choose to make this an overnight experience, there are numerous campsites along Matthews Creek—twenty-four primitive campsites and some group sites that can be reserved for ten to twenty people. Backcountry permits are available at the visitor center. To reach the Matthews Creek backcountry campsites, it is necessary to hike extra miles on the purple-blazed Dismal Trail. For those who are day hiking, this is a backtrack hike, so turn around and follow the red blazes back to US 276. An overnight loop option is featured in Hike 30.

33. Battlefield Trail

Round trip: 1.5 miles
Difficulty: Easy to moderate
Hiking time: 30 minutes
High point: 1000 feet
Elevation gain: 150 feet
Best season: Any season
Map: USGS Grover Quad
Contact: Kings Mountain National Military Park, 2625 Park Road, Blacksburg, SC 29702, (864) 936-7921

Getting there: (From Greenville, SC, 1.5 hours; from Charlotte, NC, 30 minutes) Kings Mountain National Military Park is located on Route 216 only a short drive from Charlotte, NC, and Greenville, SC. From Greenville, travel on I-85 north to NC Exit 2. From Charlotte, travel on I-85 south to NC Exit 2. The park is about 2 miles east of I-85 on Route 216, which becomes Battleground Road after 0.3 mile, then Park Road after an additional 2.2 miles.

Kings Mountain National Military Park commemorates a pivotal and significant victory by American Patriots over American Loyalists during the Southern Campaign of the Revolutionary War. The battle fought on

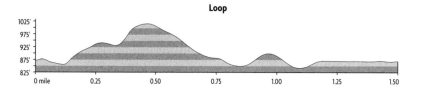

October 7, 1780, destroyed the left wing of Cornwallis's army and effectively ended Loyalist ascendance in the Carolinas. The victory halted the British advance into North Carolina, forced Lord Cornwallis to retreat from Charlotte into South Carolina, and gave General Nathanael Greene the opportunity to reorganize the American Army.

This 1.5-mile hike on the Battlefield Trail starts behind the visitor center and loops around Fergusons Cairn, the burial site of British Major Patrick Ferguson. It is marked by wayside exhibits and battle monuments that tell the story of the historic skirmish between patriot and Loyalist troops.

To hike this loop trail counterclockwise, follow the paved path from the visitor center to the trailhead, marked by a large brown-and-white metal trail sign located only a short distance from the building.

The trail quickly turns to dirt (which is much easier on your dog's paws) and ascends gradually through a hardwood forest over the first half mile to about 1000 feet. This small knob is the high point on the trail, and the park service occasionally uses prescribed burns in this area to keep the vegetation under control. Dogs will likely find the smells of charred timber interesting, and the ground may be littered with the dead and blackened timber.

From the knob, the trail descends slightly, then turns back to the southeast and eventually northeast to complete the loop back at the visitor center, which has a short film with more details on the historic battle. The

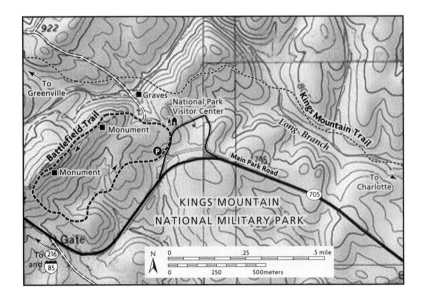

Roger Cardoe and Jim Bunting head out on the Battlefield Trail with Rebel.

route is fairly easy, with minimal elevation change, and is recommended for hikers who are looking for a leisurely stroll with their canine.

If a more challenging hike is desired, consider Browns Mountain (Hike 34), which is also located in this area.

34. Browns Mountain

Round trip: 16 miles
Difficulty: Moderate to difficult
Hiking time: 8–10 hours
High point: 1000 feet
Elevation gain: 400 feet
Best season: Any season
Map: USGS Grover Quad
Contact: Kings Mountain National Military Park, 2625 Park Road, Blacksburg, SC 29702, (864) 936-7921

Getting there: (From Greenville, SC, 1.5 hours; Charlotte, NC, 30 minutes) Kings Mountain National Military Park is located on Route 216 (becomes Park Road) only a short drive from Charlotte, NC, and Greenville, SC. From Greenville, travel on I-85 north to NC Exit 2. From

Charlotte, travel on I-85 south to NC Exit 2. The park is about 2 miles east of I-85 on Route 216.

This loop hike on the Kings Mountain National Recreational Trail includes a 0.5-mile side hike to Browns Mountain. At 1045 feet it is the highest point on the route, with decent winter views to the south and southwest. Browns Mountain was once the site of a fire tower, and the four stone pillars can still be seen on the summit where they held the foundation of the structure in place.

Kings Mountain National Recreational Trail passes along the southern portion of the Kings Mountain Range, and this 16-mile hike traverses both the Kings Mountain National Military Park and Kings Mountain State Park. The military park is the site of a prominent Revolutionary War battle (discussed in more detail in Hike 33, the Battlefield Trail) while the state park, originally built in the 1930s by the Civilian Conservation Corps, documents the lifestyles of early pioneers at the Living History Farm. The state park is designed to meet the needs of the modern-day outdoor adventurer, with recreational activities including hiking, picnicking, fishing, paddling, and horseback riding over 6883 acres of forest.

Browns Mountain can be accessed from either the national park or

Daphne, a bull mastiff owned by Christianne Curran, takes a break on a hot summer day.

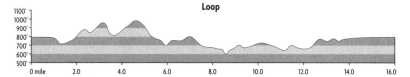

the state park, but this book describes the shorter route heading counterclockwise and starting at the Kings Mountain National Park visitor center. For the first 0.2 mile, follow the Battlefield Trail until the Kings Mountain National Recreational Trail descends slightly, then turns west and makes a gradual climb up to and across Route 216. From here, the trail descends to a small stream that is a great place for the pooch to wallow in the shallow water or slurp a healthy drink before the climb up Browns Mountain. The short 0.5-mile side hike is moderately difficult, so expect to see the hound's tongue hanging out by the time he makes it to the top. Unfortunately, there are numerous hardwoods surrounding Browns Mountain, which limit the views to the winter months.

To continue the loop, backtrack to the Kings Mountain National Recreational Trail and hike south to Garner Branch Campsite. This is one

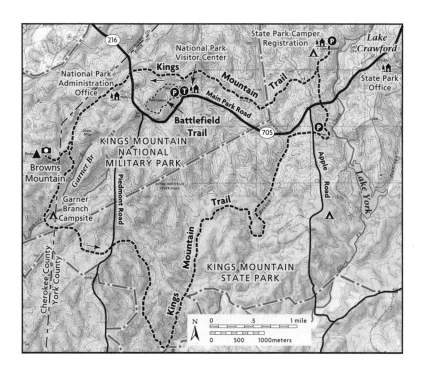

The view to the south from the summit of Browns Mountain

of only two designated campsites on the route, and it is the only site within the national park boundary. Overnight backpackers should check in with the National Park Service to firm up a reservation before they leave. The site is located on a hill just north of the state park boundary, which is marked by a cleared service road that serves as a fire break. If the national park site is full, another option is to book the designated state park campsite on Apple Road about 11.5 miles through the loop. The state park service manages this backcountry hike, so register with them before departure using the contact information listed with the Kings Mountain Nature Trail (Hike 35).

After Garner Branch Campsite, the trail crosses into the state park, descends to a small creek (the water source for the Garner Branch Campsite), and makes a hairpin turn in the southern section of the park. This is the least traveled section of trail, which occasionally gets some horse traffic (although the park service asks that horseback riders stay to the designated horse trails). If the pooch encounters a horse, make sure to secure his leash and hold him still until the horseback riders pass. This is for everyone's safety, including the dog's.

After the hairpin turn, the Kings Mountain National Recreation Trail continues northeast, crossing a few small streams (additional sources of water for the pooch), then reaches Apple Road and the state park campsite. Parking is nearby, so the national park site is definitely the better option for a true backcountry experience. However, the state park does have nice front-country facilities, including a 116-site developed campground that is open year-round if car-camping is the preference.

To complete the loop, hike north toward the state park visitor center (which also has parking facilities). Then turn west to cross the boundary back into the national park and return to the military park visitor center, where the hike started.

Although this 16-mile loop could be done as a day hike, it is recommended as either an overnight backpacking trip or an in-and-out hike to Browns Mountain, which is about 5.5 miles round trip from the national park visitor center.

35. Kings Mountain Nature Trail

Round trip: 1.2 miles
Difficulty: Easy
Hiking time: 30 minutes
High point: 850 feet
Elevation gain: 117 feet
Best season: Any season
Map: USGS Grover Quad
Contact: Kings Mountain State Park, 1277 Park Road, Blacksburg, SC 29702, (803) 222-3209

Getting there: (From Greenville, SC, 1.5 hours; from Charlotte, NC, 30 minutes) At I-85 in Kings Mountain, NC, take Exit 8. Turn left onto Route 161, go across the NC/SC state line, and the Kings Mountain State Park entrance will be on the right.

From I-77 in Rock Hill, SC, take the exit for Route 5. Follow Route 5 through Rock Hill to York. In York, travel north on Route 321, then bear left onto Route 161. The Kings Mountain State Park entrance will be on the left.

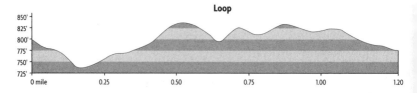

Kings Mountain State Park rests in the foothills of the Blue Ridge Mountains next to the Kings Mountain National Military Park, a prominent Revolutionary War battle site in the late 1700s (see Hike 33). A Living History Farm is located at the state park, which allows visitors to relive the lifestyles of the early pioneers through a replica of a nineteenth-century South Carolina yeoman farm. The farm includes a barn, cotton gin, and blacksmith/carpenter shop.

This easy 1.2-mile loop trail begins at the picnic area in Kings Mountain State Park (not at the national park, like the Battlefield Trail and Browns Mountain hikes featured earlier in Hikes 33 and 34). The Kings Mountain Nature Trail, a pleasant hike through a lightly forested area, is suitable for all members of the family, including the dog. This trail is not far from Charlotte, North Carolina, and is occasionally crowded on the weekends, particularly in the warmer months. So the pooch must

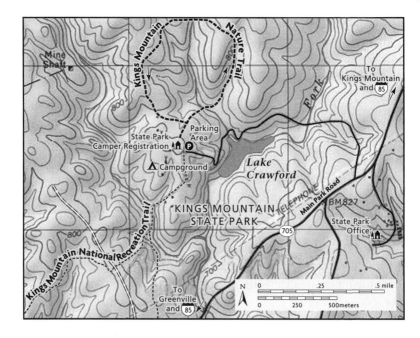

Co-author Steve Goodrich and his dog Rebel relax in the parking area after a hike in the Kings Mountain area.

be on a leash of no more than six feet, as at many of the state parks in both South Carolina and Georgia.

The trail starts north of the campground and parking lot and makes a small loop to the northwest of Lake Crawford. Some interpretive signs positioned along the trail will educate the hiker about the local wildlife, vegetation, and history of the surrounding area. The forest consists of dense hardwood with a floor covered in lush vegetation. It is especially beautiful during the spring months when colorful flowering trees and bushes are in full bloom. The pooch will undoubtedly get a snoot full of smells in this area, and may also be tempted to chase the numerous squirrels and small chipmunks that race along the forest floor here.

Continuing counterclockwise, the route brings you back around to the parking area where you began.

NORTHERN/ CENTRAL SOUTH CAROLINA

36. Lake Haigler Trail

Round trip: 1.5 miles
Difficulty: Easy
Hiking time: 1 hour
High point: 640 feet
Elevation gain: 85 feet
Best season: Any season
Map: USGS Fort Mill Quad
Contact: Anne Springs Close Greenway, P.O. Box 1209, Fort Mill, SC
    29716, (803) 548-7252

Getting there: (From Atlanta, GA, 4 hours; from Charlotte, NC, 30 minutes) In Charlotte, take I-77 south 9 miles. Exit onto Route 160 and drive east toward Fort Mill. After 1 mile, turn left on the US 21 Bypass and continue 1.5 miles. The park entrance is on the right.

The Anne Springs Close Greenway is a nature preserve opened in 1995 by members of the Close family who have owned the land for over 200 years. The 2300-acre Greenway, located just south of Charlotte, North Carolina, is a beautiful park-like facility that is managed with no assistance from the federal or state government. Annual memberships and day-use fees currently provide the funding to operate the park.

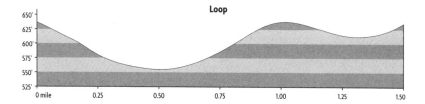

Known as the Great Wagon Road, Nation Ford Road, which runs northeast from Lake Haigler, lies within the Anne Springs Close Greenway. European settlers developed this path in the early years of our nation, and learned the route from the Catawba Indians who valued it as an ancient trading route. During the Civil War, the Greenway also hosted Jefferson Davis, who used a plantation home at the northern part of the park as the final meeting place of his cabinet prior to the end of the Civil War.

Today, the Anne Springs Close Greenway is primarily valued by outdoor enthusiasts who enjoy the opportunities to hike, fish, mountain bike, camp, and horseback ride in the park. The Lake Haigler Trail is one of two hikes in the park (see also the Springfield Trail, Hike 37).

This easy 1.5-mile loop hike around Lake Haigler starts at the parking area near the nature center. Located in the center of the park, the best way to reach the nature center is to enter the park through the Dairy

One of eight primitive campsites on the north side of Lake Haigler

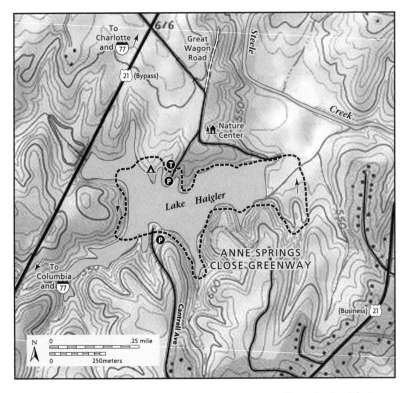

Barn entrance off US 21 Business. The route is well marked with interpretive signs that help detail the flora and fauna native to this part of South Carolina.

The hike is profiled in a counterclockwise direction, so walk south from the nature center and turn right once the trail reaches Lake Haigler. The lake is stocked with bass, catfish, and carp, and is popular for fishing. You may see some fishermen during the hike, and the pooch should respect their interest in casting along the banks—although it may be difficult for a dog to resist wading along the shore.

After a short distance, hike around the western side of Lake Haigler. There are two bridges in this area that traverse arms of the lake, and hikers can enjoy some fantastic views of Lake Haigler from them. The trail heads east after the second bridge along the southern shore of the lake, then loops back to the north across the dam and spillway for the lake. The nature center is only a short distance from here, so turn to the west and complete the loop.

Hikers are allowed on all trails in the park, including the mountain

A view of Lake Haigler from the trail

biking and horseback riding trails. Anne Springs Close Greenway requires that dogs be leashed at all times to protect the nesting birds and other animals in the park.

37. Springfield Trail

Round trip: 2.3 miles
Difficulty: Easy
Hiking time: 1–2 hours
High point: 700 feet
Elevation gain: 136 feet
Best season: Any season
Map: USGS Fort Mill Quad
Contact: Anne Springs Close Greenway, P.O. Box 1209, Fort Mill, SC 29716, (803) 548-7252

Getting there: (From Atlanta, GA, 4 hours; from Charlotte, NC, 30 minutes) In Charlotte, NC, take I-77 south 9 miles. Exit onto Route 160 and

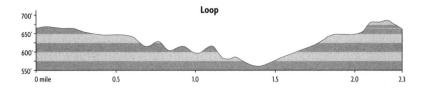

drive east toward Fort Mill. After 1 mile, turn left on the US 21 Bypass and continue 1.5 miles. The Anne Springs Close Greenway entrance is on the right.

The Springfield Trail is one of two hikes featured in the Anne Springs Close Greenway, located near Rock Hill, South Carolina (see also the Lake Haigler Trail, Hike 36), and the highlight is a suspension bridge over Steele Creek in the southern portion of the loop.

From the Dairy Barn, leave the trailhead and hike counterclockwise, heading south. You may notice a few mountain bikers on the trail (who

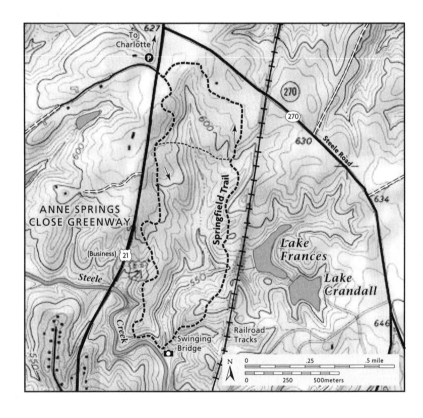

A log cabin built by the Rev. Billy Graham's grandfather is located in the Anne Springs Close Greenway.

also share this route), so keep the dog leashed to avoid any unwelcome collisions. The trail is wide enough to accommodate both parties, so sharing the route shouldn't be an issue.

The Springfield Trail climbs a short knob, then descends gradually to a swinging bridge at Steele Creek about halfway through the hike at 550 feet. The wooden structure is exciting to cross and may have the hound pondering the situation, but the views of the stream are therapeutic and it's a nice break on the hike. Look for white oak, hickory, and pine trees, which are common in this area and grow along the forest that surrounds Steele Creek. Then turn back to the north and complete the loop.

As this book was going to press, the Greenway had closed the eastern portion of the route. So this may end up as an in-and-out hike to the swinging bridge. Check with the Anne Springs Close Greenway for current trail conditions before you depart.

38. Landsford Canal

Distance: 1.5 miles one-way (shuttle hike)
Difficulty: Easy
Hiking time: 1 hour
High point: 530 feet
Elevation gain: Negligible
Best season: Any season
Map: USGS Catawba Quad
Contact: Landsford Canal State Historic Site, 2051 Park Drive
    Catawba, SC 29704, (803) 789-5800

Getting there: (From Columbia, SC, 1 hour; from Charlotte, NC, 30 minutes) In Columbia, take I-77 to Exit 65 and head east on Route 9. After 1.2 miles, turn left onto Route 223 and drive 6.7 miles. Turn left onto US 21 and continue for 2 miles to Landsford Road (Route 327). Turn right onto Landsford Road and drive 2 miles to Park Drive (Route 690) where you turn left to enter the park. The northern trailhead is 0.5 mile into the park, in the picnic area.

From Charlotte, NC, take I-77 to Exit 77 and turn left onto Route 21. Continue for 15 miles on US 21, then turn left onto Landsford Road (Route 327). The park entrance is 1.5 miles ahead on the left. Turn onto Park Drive and drive 0.5 mile to the picnic area and the northern trailhead.

To reach the southern section of the Landsford Canal State Historic Site, start at the junction of Park Drive and Landsford Road (Route 327) and head south on Route 327 to Canal Road (Route 330). At Canal Road, turn left and head east toward the Catawba River. The southern trailhead is located at the end of the road along the river.

Landsford Canal was once an important trading route running from the coast to the foothills of South Carolina. It was built in 1820 by Robert Leckie as a canal lock designed to avoid the rough waters of the nearby Catawba River. The lock did not operate long, however, due to continual problems with flooding, but today is one of only a handful of canals in the state that have survived without structural damage. The Landsford

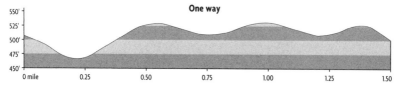

Canal State Historic Site was created to protect this unique structure, and it operates five days a week, with operations running Thursday through Monday from 9 AM until 6 PM year-round. The canal is dry under normal conditions, but occasionally holds some water in a few areas. The lockkeeper's house, located near the northern trailhead at the park, serves as an interpretive center to educate the public on the historical significance of Landsford Canal.

This one-way, shuttle hike at the Landsford Canal State Historic Site is actually comprised of two trails, the Nature Trail and the Canal Trail, both marked with interpretive signs. The Nature Trail is a short path that runs parallel to the Canal Trail over the first 0.5 mile to the east. Hikers and

A view of the Catawba River from the trail

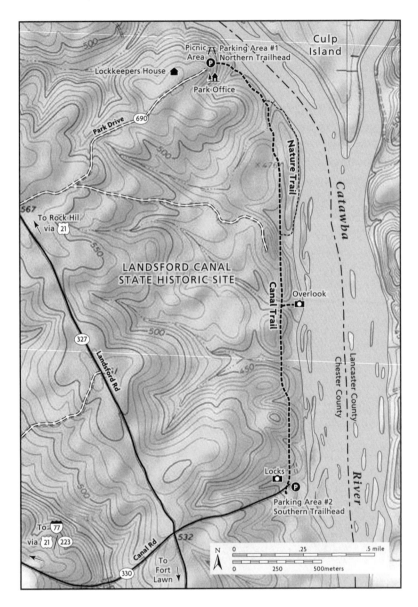

their dogs have the option of following either route, and may consider alternating between the two for an in-and-out hike of 3 total miles.

The walk begins at the north end of the Nature Trail, then heads south with very little elevation change. After a short distance, the Nature Trail and Canal Trail temporarily part ways but rejoin after about 0.5 mile.

There is a viewing area just south of this junction, designed for the observation of spider lilies, wildflowers that thrive in the humid conditions typical here in late May and early June. Steps lead to the viewing area (which may be an interesting climb for smaller dogs), and the observation site is a nice break—especially during the spring when the wildflowers are in full bloom.

The Canal Trail continues to the canal locks and onto a stone bridge just past the viewing area as it approaches the southern trailhead after 1.5 miles. Hikers complete the one-way shuttle hike at the parking area on Canal Road (but can backtrack to the northern trailhead for a 3-mile hike, round trip).

The park is currently designated as a day-use facility, which means no campgrounds or backcountry campsites are developed in the Landsford Canal area. Nonetheless, the historic site is a great place to spend the day, and both you and your pet will enjoy the easy terrain and views out to the Catawba River.

39. Garden of the Waxhaws

Round trip: 1.0 mile
Difficulty: Easy
Hiking time: 30 minutes
High point: 570 feet
Elevation gain: 55 feet
Best season: Any season
Map: USGS Van Wyck Quad
Contact: Andrew Jackson State Park, 196 Andrew Jackson Road, Lancaster, SC, 29720, (803) 285-3344

Getting there: (From Atlanta, GA, 4 hours; from Charlotte, NC, 20 minutes) In Lancaster, SC, head north on US 521 for 8 miles to the Andrew Jackson State Park entrance on the right. Enter the park and veer left at

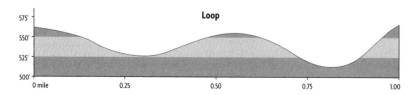

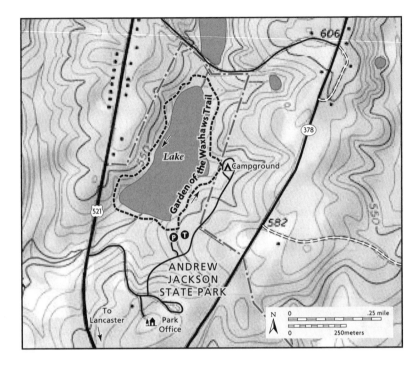

the fork. At the gravel road, turn left and park at the lake. The trailhead is near the fishing dock.

Andrew Jackson State Park is named for the former president who lived most of his young life in this area and is honored by a statue created by Anna Hyatt Huntington, which is located a short distance from the park office. As a famous sculptress with a summer home nearby (see Hike 54), Anna made the statue of the young president and gave it to the children of South Carolina to commemorate this legendary leader.

The land that houses the park was given to the state of South Carolina by the county in the 1950s. The 360-acre facility contains a museum (which documents the lives of early settlers), a campground, a playground, a meetinghouse, a boat dock, and a lake stocked with bass, brim, and catfish.

The short, 1-mile Garden of the Waxhaws Trail begins at the fishing dock and is a loop hike that winds around a lake (not shown on the USGS topos) in the northern section of the park. It is straightforward,

Rebel enjoys a swim in the lake on a hot afternoon in early summer.

well marked with interpretive signs, and great for older or smaller dogs that prefer an easy day on the trail. Hikers who appreciate a leisurely afternoon on the trail will also enjoy the gentle terrain of this trail.

Start by hiking counterclockwise past the boat dock, heading north along the lake. In a few minutes, you may hear the sights and sounds of the park campground, a short distance away. Keep the pooch on a leash (as required by the park) so your pet doesn't wander off to sniff down a camper's grill.

The trail continues in a northerly direction for about 0.5 mile, then makes a hairpin turn around the upper edge of the lake and curves south toward the dam. You might choose to let the dog wade briefly in the shallow end of the lake before turning south, especially on a hot summer day.

At roughly the 0.8-mile mark, the trail meets the dam where hikers cross a grassy causeway and return to the parking area where the trail started. There are no backcountry campsites on this route, but Andrew Jackson State Park has twenty-five campsites for those who plan to make this an overnight venture.

40. Crawford Hiking Trail

Round trip: 1.1 miles
Difficulty: Easy
Hiking time: 30 minutes
High point: 625 feet
Elevation gain: 75 feet
Best season: Any season
Map: USGS Van Wyck Quad
Contact: Andrew Jackson State Park, 196 Andrew Jackson Road,
   Lancaster, SC, 29720, (803) 285-3344

Getting there: (From Atlanta, GA, 4 hours; from Charlotte, NC, 30 minutes) In Lancaster, SC, head north on US 521 for 8 miles to the Andrew Jackson State Park entrance. Drive to the end of the road and park. The trailhead is near the Meeting House.

Andrew Jackson State Park is located near Rock Hill, South Carolina, and the Crawford Trail is one of two hikes featured in the park. (For

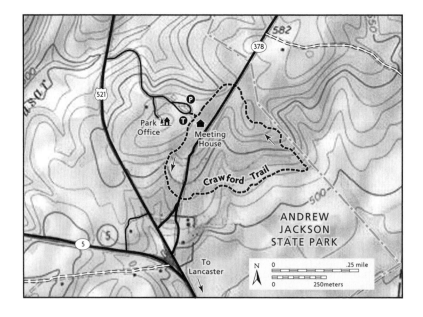

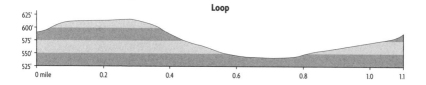

more information on the park, see Hike 39.)

The short Crawford Hiking Trail loop is a 1.1-mile hike that begins near the parking area to the right of the Meeting House. The trail leads through a picnic area in the southeastern corner of the park where it crosses Route 378 on two occasions before winding back to the starting point.

As you leave the trailhead hiking counterclockwise, the terrain is gentle with very little elevation change, and a canopy of pines provides some cover and gentle conditions for the pooch's feet. After 0.3 mile, the trail descends slightly for about 75 feet as it turns east and bottoms out around the 0.7-mile mark. Here the trail opens up briefly to an area occasionally filled with wildflowers including honeysuckle and sweet gum. Your dog might want to stop and take in the interesting smells here before making a modest climb back up and across Route 378 to

Rebel begs for some handouts from Roger Cardoe during a late dinner at the campsite.

the Meeting House and parking area where the loop began.

For those wishing to make this an overnight adventure, there are twenty-five campsites in Andrew Jackson State Park. Dogs are permitted in the campsites as long as they are on a leash of no longer than six feet and are under voice command at all times.

41. Cheraw Nature Trail

Round trip: 2 miles
Difficulty: Easy
Hiking time: 1 hour
High point: 250 feet
Elevation gain: 90 feet
Best season: Any season
Maps: USGS Cheraw and Cash Quads
Contact: Cheraw State Park, 100 State Park Road, Cheraw, SC 29520, (843) 537-9656

Getting there: (From Charlotte, NC, 1.5 hours; from Florence, SC, 40 minutes) At I-95 in Florence, take US 52/US 1 for 37 miles and drive north to the Cheraw State Park entrance. From the first stop sign in the

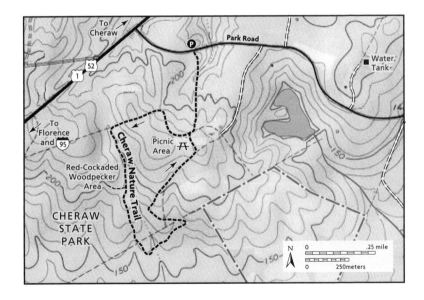

park, turn right and continue 1 mile past the golf clubhouse to reach the trailhead, on the left.

Cheraw State Park is South Carolina's oldest state park with a wealth of outdoor activities including hiking and biking trails, boating, fishing, equestrian trails, and even a championship eighteen-hole golf course. The Cheraw Nature Trail, one of two hikes in the park, is a short, 2-mile loop hike that shares part of the route with the longer Turkey Oak Trail (see Hike 42). The red-blazed Cheraw Nature Trail starts south of the main park road and is a nice, relaxing day hike for the pooch, winding through a mix of pine and oak wilderness. The loop is lightly traveled, so there will be very little congestion and lots of solitude for hikers and their pets.

From the park road, the trail departs the parking area and heads south through an area with shade trees—a major bonus in the summer months. After a short distance, the Nature Trail intersects with the loop portion of this route, where you can hike in either direction. This profile is shown heading counterclockwise, so turn to the right and within the first mile notice a short spur trail. This spur leads to the Red-Cockaded Woodpecker Area, a natural habitat for these unique birds. The brief side hike provides a nice break where you can read the interpretive signs and learn about the wildlife native to this area. The pooch may appreciate a break, too, and a well-deserved opportunity to rest the paws.

Back on the Nature Trail, the route continues west and south, making a diamond-shaped loop. Roughly halfway through the loop, the Nature Trail passes the white-blazed Turkey Oak Trail to the right on two occasions (see map for Hike 42). Stay with the red blazes to avoid 2 extra miles on the Turkey Oak Trail. After passing the second junction with the Turkey Oak Trail, the Nature Trail takes a long and hard turn back to the northeast (or left), where it eventually heads north and finishes at the main park road where it started.

There are no backcountry campsites on this loop, but those wishing to make this an overnight adventure can stay at one of the seventeen

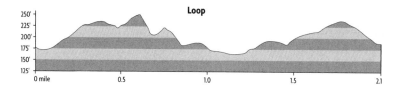

Steve and Elizabeth Cobb enjoy a day on the trail with their golden retriever, Katie.

campsites in the park. Although Cheraw State Park has eight cabins, dogs are not allowed in them, so the campsites are your best option for overnight accommodations.

42. Turkey Oak Trail

Round trip: 4 miles
Difficulty: Easy
Hiking time: 2–3 hours
High point: 250 feet
Elevation gain: 125 feet
Best season: Any season
Maps: USGS Cheraw and Cash Quads
Contact: Cheraw State Park, 100 State Park Road, Cheraw, SC 29520, (843) 537-9656

Getting there: From I-95 in Florence, SC, take US 52 and drive 37 miles north to the Cheraw State Park entrance. From the first stop sign in the park, turn right and continue 1 mile past the golf clubhouse to reach the trailhead.

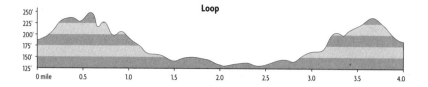

The Turkey Oak Trail is one of two hikes featured in Cheraw State Park, located near Cheraw, South Carolina (see also the Cheraw Nature Trail, Hike 41, for more information on this wilderness). The Turkey Oak Trail is one of the newest hiking trails in the state, and is an extension of the Cheraw Nature Trail.

The 4-mile loop hike starts at the parking area and is profiled here in a counterclockwise direction. Start the hike by walking along the Cheraw Nature Trail, following red blazes and heading south.

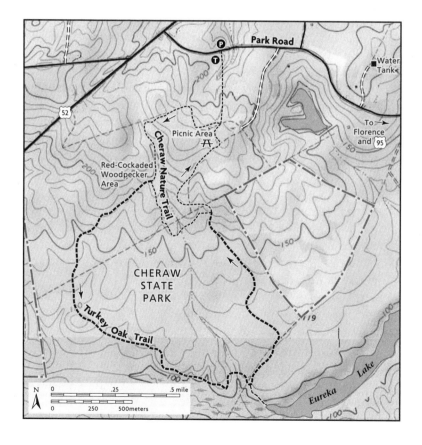

Susan Schuffenhauer and her husky, Indy, relax in a grassy area just off the trail.

In the first 0.5 mile, the trail ascends gradually, then begins a 100-foot descent toward the Turkey Oak Trail. Along the way there is a short spur trail leading to the Red-Cockaded Woodpecker Area, a worthwhile side trip if time is available. Otherwise, continue to meet up with the white-blazed Turkey Oak Trail and begin a 2-mile loop that turns down toward Eureka Lake, then switches back to the north to meet up again with the Cheraw Nature Trail.

To hike to Eureka Lake, look for a bench along the Turkey Oak Trail. There is a second spur trail here that leads to the water, which may also provide a welcome drink for your pet. You may notice ducks cruising the shallows along the lake, so tighten up the hound's leash. These birds have been known to spark some interest in a dog—particularly retrievers like the golden or Labrador retriever.

From Eureka Lake, return to the Turkey Oak Trail, hike northeast back to the Cheraw Nature Trail, and make your way up a hundred feet to the trailhead at the main park road.

Hikers wishing to trim mileage on this route should consider the Cheraw Nature Trail, profiled in Hike 41. Overnight backpackers might consider the seventeen campsites and eight cabins (where no dogs are permitted) in the state park since no backcountry campsites are on this trail.

43. Stewardship Trail

Round trip: 3 miles
Difficulty: Easy
Hiking time: 2 hours
High point: 310 feet
Elevation gain: 130 feet
Best season: Spring, fall, winter
Map: USGS Columbia Northeast Quad
Contact: Harbison State Forest, 5500 Broad River Road, Columbia,
   SC 29212, (803) 896-8890, *www.state.sc.us/forest*

Getting there: (From Atlanta, GA, 3 hours; from Charleston, SC, 1.5 hours) In downtown Columbia, SC, take I-126/26 northwest toward Spartanburg. At the Piney Grove exit, head right for 1 mile, then turn left onto Broad River Road (US 176). Harbison State Forest is 1 mile ahead on the right. (See the map for the Learning Trail, Hike 44.) Parking Area 6 is 2 miles inside the park, about 0.4 mile past Parking Area 5.

Harbison State Forest is composed of 2177 acres and over 20 miles of trails ranging in length from 0.4 mile to 5.8 miles. In 1997, the Harbison Environmental Education Center was established to provide a setting for teaching about natural resources and the environment. The park is a peaceful escape from the bustling capital of South Carolina, located only a short distance away in Columbia, and visitors can view a working sawmill, check out a nineteenth-century steam loader, or visit a small fire tower as they stroll around the grounds behind the education center. Several trails and outdoor classrooms are located in the pine and hardwood forest that surround the center, making this an ideal setting for visitors to learn in a natural environment. The park is well maintained

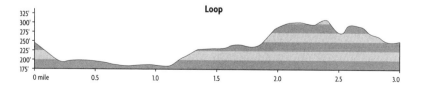

and managed, and mountain bikers, nature enthusiasts, and hikers with their dogs will all enjoy the area.

The Stewardship Trail is one of three featured hikes in Harbison State Forest (see also Hikes 44 and 45). There are many pine and maple trees along this route, and the trail is part of a project known as Forest Stewardship, which teaches responsible land-use management in the wilderness. There are several projects along the route demonstrating these principles, and this area is also known for some of the best wildlife sightings in the state forest.

To begin this loop, drive to Parking Area 6, located in the northernmost section of the state forest, and hike in a counterclockwise direction, following the green blazes.

In the first mile, the trail makes a rapid descent to the Broad River at about 175 feet. Much of the forest in this area was destroyed in 1997 by the southern pine beetle. There are several benches and a short spur trail leading to the river here, and many people take a rest stop along the Broad River to enjoy the ensuing views and the tranquility of the water.

Since the Broad River is the highlight of the Stewardship Trail, some hikers backtrack to Parking Area 6. This 3-mile loop hike is a pleasant stroll, however, and the pooch will likely appreciate the extra time on the trail. So from the river, begin a long and sometimes steep climb to 300 feet as the route turns west and crosses a small knob. Here the route turns

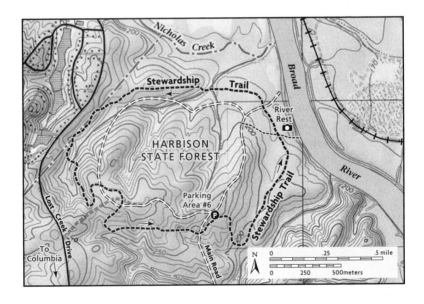

The historic Tom Bailey Saw Mill, located only a few hundred feet from the Education Center Office, in Harbison State Forest

southwest and circles back the remaining 2 miles to the parking lot.

Like the Midlands Mountain Trail (Hike 45), this loop is open to mountain bikers, but the trail is wide enough that hikers should not fear sharing the path. Keep the hound on a leash to avoid any collisions, and if you hear a mountain biker coming, step off the trail, be courteous, and wait for them to pass. Remember that bikers have the right-of-way.

44. Learning Trail

Round trip: 0.7 mile
Difficulty: Easy
Hiking time: 20 minutes
High point: 300 feet
Elevation gain: 75 feet
Best season: Fall, winter, spring
Map: USGS Columbia Northeast Quad
Contact: Harbison State Forest, 5500 Broad River Road, Columbia, SC 29212, (803) 896-8890, *www.state.sc.us/forest*

Getting there: (From Atlanta, GA, 3 hours; from Charleston, SC, 1.5 hours) In downtown Columbia, SC, take I-126/26 northwest toward

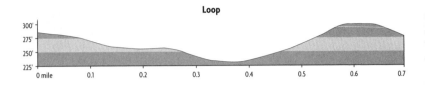

Spartanburg. Exit at the Piney Grove exit and head right for 1 mile, then turn left onto Broad River Road (US 176). Harbison State Forest is 1 mile ahead on the right.

Harbison State Forest is located near Columbia, South Carolina, and the Learning Trail is one of three hikes featured in the park. (For more information on Harbison State Forest, see the Stewardship Trail, Hike 43.)

The Learning Trail is a short, interpretive, loop trail that starts at the education center. The route, blazed in lime green, makes a small loop to the north and returns to the parking area where it began. Along the Learning Trail, park personnel have posted interpretive signs that provide insight into the various plants and animals that are native to the area.

A short distance from the education center is a vernal pond, which collects water in the spring but dries up during the hot summer months.

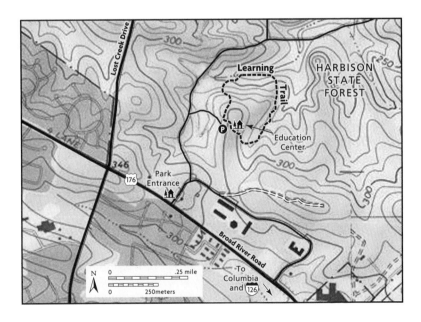

One of a number of interpretive signs on the Learning Trail in Harbison State Forest

It is important habitat for many of the animals in this Southern forest, and your pooch may find the pond quite inviting—especially in the wetter months. Unfortunately, it is off-limits to both man and beast. So please keep your dog on a leash while on the trail or around the education center, as required by the Harbison State Forest. There is a public water source at the education center, which also provides a free trail map.

About halfway through the hike, the red-blazed Discovery Trail cuts across the Learning Trail loop. Make sure to follow the lime blazes as you wind along a series of small streams and bridges. This trail is a very pleasant and easy way to spend a half hour, but if a more challenging hike is desired, consider the Midlands Mountain Trail (Hike 45) or Stewardship Trail (Hike 43). Also, keep in mind that this is a day-use facility and no camping is permitted in the Harbison State Forest.

45. Midlands Mountain Trail

Round trip: 3.7 miles
Difficulty: Moderate to difficult
Hiking time: 2 hours
High point: 310 feet
Elevation gain: 135 feet
Best season: Fall, winter, spring
Map: USGS Columbia Northeast Quad
Contact: Harbison State Forest, 5500 Broad River Road, Columbia,
    SC 29212, (803) 896-8890, *www.state.sc.us/forest*

Getting there: (From Atlanta, GA, 3 hours; from Charleston, SC, 1.5 hours) In downtown Columbia, SC, follow I-126/26 northwest toward Spartanburg. Take the Piney Grove exit and head right for 1 mile, then turn left onto Broad River Road (US 176). Harbison State Forest is 1 mile ahead on the right. Parking Area 5 is on the right 1.6 miles in from the main gate.

The Midlands Mountain Trail is one of three hikes featured in the Harbison State Forest, located near Columbia, South Carolina. (For more information on Harbison State Forest, see the Stewardship Trail, Hike 43.) This route makes a loop in the eastern portion of the state forest along the Broad River. There is no water source along the trail, although hikers and dogs can fill up on drinking water at the education center before heading out.

From Parking Area 5, the hike begins with a steep ascent to a ridge at nearly 300 feet, where the trail intersects with an old forest road that runs north-to-south. After you and the pooch catch your breath, turn left onto the dirt road and head northeast for a short distance to hike this loop clockwise.

As the trail turns to the east, it crosses a series of small knobs that

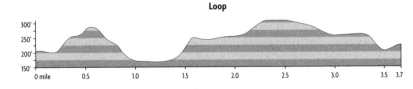

occasionally have views of the Broad River. From here, descend gradually to the river and pass a side trail for mountain bikers, located to the right. This cut-off trail (normally reserved for bikers) is a designated alternative for hikers and their dogs during periods of extremely wet weather or when the Broad River floods its banks and muddy conditions exist. Otherwise, hikers should follow the blue blazes to stay on the Midlands Mountain Trail, which continues straight ahead, then makes a sharp turn to the south along the Broad River. Keep dogs leashed at all times on this hike, since mountain bikers are permitted to use both sections of trail and are as eager to avoid a collision as you are.

The Midlands Mountain Trail drops to 175 feet as it follows the river for a half mile, then climbs steeply for about 100 feet to another knob that forms a saddle with an area called Harbison Bluffs. During the climb, the cut-off trail of the Midlands Mountain route appears again on the right. From here, you'll have glimpses of the Broad River running north-to-south.

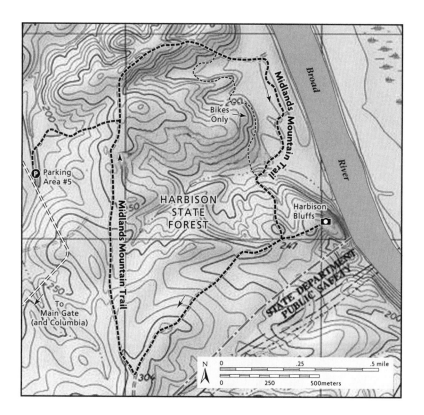

A fire tower near the Education Center at Harbison State Forest

About 0.3 mile past the cut-off, just after a steep 75-foot climb, is a spur trail leading 0.2 miles to the cliffs at Harbison Bluffs, which offer a spectacular 180-degree view. This vista makes the Midlands Mountain Trail one of the best hikes in the park, but watch the pooch carefully since it is at least 100 feet down to the river from the bluffs.

To complete the Midlands Mountain loop, backtrack from Harbison Bluffs, hiking southwest and gradually gaining elevation to another small knob at 304 feet. Here the trail makes a hard turn to the right and descends back to the trail that leads to Parking Area 5 (now on the left).

SOUTHERN SOUTH CAROLINA

46. Oakridge and Kingsnake Trails

Round trip: 11.1 miles
Difficulty: Moderate
Hiking time: 4 hours
High point: 100 Feet
Elevation gain: Negligible
Best season: Spring, fall, winter
Maps: USGS Gadsden and Wateree Quads
Contact: Congaree National Park, 100 National Park Road,
Hopkins, SC 29061, (803) 776-4396

Getting there: (From Charleston, SC, 2 hours; from Columbia, SC, 20 minutes) In Columbia, take I-77 south to Exit 5 (Bluff Road). Travel on Bluff Road southeast, following signs toward the national monument. After 12 miles, the road will fork with Old Bluff Road. Continue on Bluff Road another 6.2 miles and turn right on South Cedar Creek Road (Route 1288). Continue another 2 miles to the Kingsnake trailhead parking area.

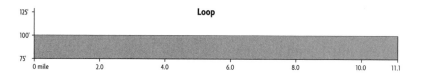

Congaree National Park is the largest preserve of old-growth floodplain forest in the United States. Located along the Congaree River near Columbia, South Carolina, the park was designated an International Biosphere Reserve in 1983, and it has some of the largest trees that can be seen in the eastern United States.

Along the Congaree River, which runs from west to east just south of here, the trail conditions vary with the weather. After severe rains, the trails flood and occasionally become impassable. The ranger station typically has up-to-date information, so make sure to check with them before you head out on any of the 20 miles of trail in the park. Also, keep in mind that there are 2 miles of elevated boardwalks in the park that do not permit dogs.

The Oakridge and Kingsnake Trails can be combined for an 11.1-mile loop hike, described here. However, the Kingsnake Trail can be done as an in-and-out hike if you are looking for a shorter route, which cuts the mileage to 7.4 miles total. Regardless, this hike starts at the parking area for the Kingsnake Trail off Route 1288. The trail heads south through a mix of heavy forest and marsh and follows orange blazes.

The feral hog has done well in this rustic habitat, so don't be surprised to see one tearing at the ground with its tusks as you wander through the wilderness. These untamed animals (also known as wild pigs) have existed in the United States since the 1500s when they were introduced in Florida. While many national parks have undertaken programs to

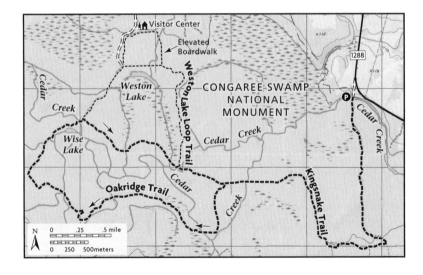

Cedar Creek as it appears farther down stream after a heavy rain

control their numbers, some are still present in this area. If the pooch catches their scent, hold the leash tight. These feral hogs can tear your hound apart with their strong tusks, and the damage they cause to the forest as they root for insects has made them a nuisance to many forest professionals.

After about 1.3 miles, the trail runs adjacent to Cedar Creek and makes a turn to the west. Cedar Creek flows east through the majority of the park and eventually connects with the Congaree River. Watch for snakes in this area, especially along Cedar Creek. Snakes are so widespread in the park that most hikers see at least one during their hike (another good reason to keep your dog on a leash).

About 3.7 miles from the trailhead, the Kingsnake Trail meets up with the red-blazed Oakridge Trail and makes a loop shared with the yellow-blazed Weston Lake Loop Trail. Here you have the option of turning back for a 7.4-mile in-and-out hike, or completing the loop for an 11.1-mile round trip.

The forest here is thick, and wildlife is rampant. The critters are usually the most active in the early-morning or late-evening hours, and it is no coincidence that the insects (and especially the mosquitoes) are also active at this time. Insect repellent is recommended year round, but it is critical in the summer months. Consider getting the pooch treated with Advantix, Frontline, or some type of flea, tick, and insect preventive before you hit the trail. Your canine companion will have a much more enjoyable experience as a result.

About 3 miles from the start of the loop at Route 1288, turn left onto the Oakridge Trail, and hike clockwise for approximately 2.5 miles, passing Wise Lake. Here the trail crosses Cedar Creek and meets up with the yellow-blazed Weston Lake Loop Trail, which leads off the route to the visitor center for Congaree National Park. Stay right and continue east on the combined Oakridge and Weston Lake Loop Trails for a short distance before crossing another creek after about a mile near a second junction with the Weston Lake Loop Trail, on the left. Continue walking east for about 0.5 mile and return to the orange-blazed Kingsnake Trail, which backtracks to the trailhead.

The Oakridge and Kingsnake Trails offer an excellent opportunity to leave behind the crowds that typically gather near the visitor center. This section of the park offers a unique look at the wilderness of the Congaree River basin, and you can expect a lot of solitude on this route. Although there are no backcountry campsites on the loop, there is a small primitive "after-hours" campsite just inside the park. Check with the park service for details.

47. Oak Pinolley Trail

Round trip: 1 mile
Difficulty: Easy
Hiking time: 30 minutes
High point: 94 feet
Elevation gain: Negligible
Best season: Any season
Map: USGS Saint Paul Quad
Contact: Santee State Park, 251 State Park Road, Santee, SC 29142, (803) 854-2408

Getting there: (From Columbia, SC, 1 hour; from Charleston, SC, 1 hour) At Exit 98 on I-95 at Santee, drive west on Route 6 for 1.2 miles and turn right onto State Park Road (Orangeburg County S-38-105). At

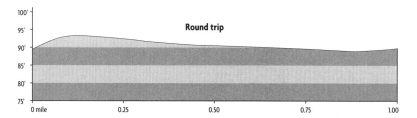

the stop sign go straight on State Park Road to the north trailhead at the Cypress View Playground. (For an overall view of the the park, see the map for Hike 48.)

Best known for its striped bass fishing, Santee State Park is one of the most popular state parks in South Carolina. The park offers 2500 acres of flooded wilderness that include miles of shoreline on Lake Marion and recreation trails for both hikers and mountain bikers. The lake was created in 1949 when 100,000 acres were flooded to provide electric power for the Southeast. This makes Santee State Park a birdwatchers' paradise, with quail, brown thrasher, and Carolina wren among the numerous species of birds that reside here.

There are three loop trails for hikers and their dogs to enjoy in Santee State Park (see also Hikes 48 and 49). The Oak Pinolley Trail is a 1-mile

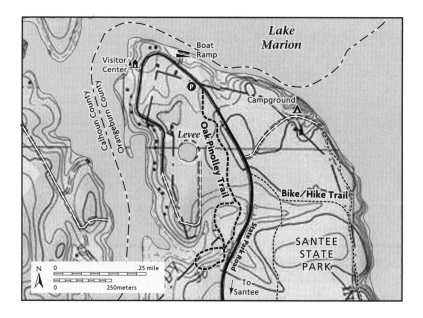

A view of Marion Lake from the visitor center at Santee State Park

loop in the northwestern corner of the park and is the most easily accessed of the trails at Santee State Park, since it starts very close to the visitor center. There is a small exhibit area in the visitor center showcasing some of the wildlife in the park. Day hikers should check out the display, pick up a trail map, and load up on drinking water before heading out, since there is none available on the trail. This is also a good time to put a leash on the pooch, as required by the park.

At the playground on State Park Road, leave the trailhead for the yellow-blazed Oak Pinolley Trail and head south, hugging the main road. After a short distance, the trail makes a short loop and crosses a small bridge. Hike in either direction, then complete the loop and backtrack to the trailhead where you started.

Like the Limestone Nature Trail (Hike 49), this hike is ideal for older or smaller dogs that want a relaxing jaunt in the wilderness. Although the route is close to some popular facilities in the park, it still makes for a pleasant stroll through the forest. If you and the pooch are contemplating a more challenging hike, consider the Santee Bike/Hike Trail to the east (Hike 48).

Santee State Park does not offer backcountry campsites, but has 158 drive-in campsites that are available to hikers and their pets. The thirty cabins in the park are off-limits to dogs, and they are not permitted in or around these buildings.

48. Santee Bike/Hike Trail

Round trip: 7.5 miles
Difficulty: Moderate
Hiking time: 3–4 hours
High point: 135 feet
Elevation gain: 45 feet
Best season: Any season
Map: USGS Saint Paul Quad
Contact: Santee State Park, 251 State Park Road, Santee, SC 29142, (803) 854-2408

Getting there: (From Columbia, SC, 1 hour; from Charleston, SC, 1 hour) From Exit 98 on I-95 at Santee, drive west on Route 6 for 1.2 miles and turn right onto State Park Road (Orangeburg County S-38-105). At the stop sign you can go straight on State Park Road to the north trailhead at the Cypress View Playground, where this hike begins, or turn right onto Cleveland Road and go to the south trailhead at the swimming area.

The Santee Bike/Hike Trail is one of three loop trails located in Santee State Park. (For more information on Santee State Park, see the Oak Pinolley Trail, Hike 47.) This blue-blazed 7.5-mile route is shared between hikers and mountain bikers, although the wide and well-worn path allows plenty of room for both groups.

The Santee Bike/Hike Trail has spectacular views of Lake Marion to the east, and is relatively flat which makes it fairly easy despite being the longest trail in the park. The hike begins at the trailhead just before

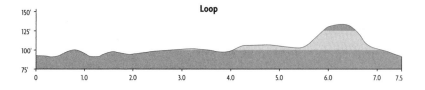

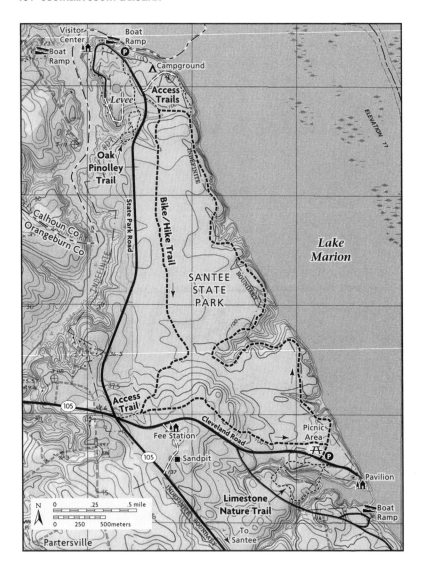

the entrance to the camping area on State Park Road, at the north end of the park. Follow the trail in a counterclockwise direction, heading south along the park road through a forest of pines and hardwoods that are occasionally draped with Spanish moss.

After a few miles, the Bike/Hike Trail approaches Cleveland Road and parallels it for about 2 miles, heading east. On the right, hikers will notice an access trail to State Park Road in the southeastern corner of the

An access trail to the hike/bike trail near the junction of State Park Road and Cleveland Road, in the southwestern corner of the park

park near Route 105, which makes for a shorter shuttle hike if desired. Otherwise, continue east toward Lake Marion, then turn north to hug the shore as you approach another access point off Cleveland Road near a picnic area.

The final few miles of trail follow the shores of Lake Marion. Goldens, Labs, and other water dogs may be tempted by the lake, but alligators inhabit the water—so stay on the trail, and keep a leash on your pet at all times. Mountain bikers will appreciate this gesture as well, since they have no desire to collide with a wandering canine.

In several places along Lake Marion, the trail opens to sweeping views of the water and to the ghostly images of dead trees and cypress stumps left from the 1949 flood. Some spur trails lead from the main loop to the lake, and the side trip is well worth the effort—particularly in the early morning as the sun rises in the east.

This trail is best hiked in the late fall through early spring, since insects are abundant in the summer months. Take insect repellent during periods of warm weather, and carry plenty of water. Lake Marion is brackish, which means it has a mix of fresh and salt water, so load up at the Santee State Park visitor center before heading out.

For those wishing to make this an overnight adventure, Santee State Park has 174 dog-friendly campsites for hikers who want to spend the night, but the thirty cabins (some of which are situated over the water) are off-limits to pets. There are no backcountry campsites on the Santee Bike/Hike Trail or on any trail in the park.

49. Limestone Nature Trail

Round trip: 0.8 mile
Difficulty: Easy
Hiking time: 30 minutes
High point: 95 feet
Elevation gain: Negligible
Best season: Any season
Map: USGS Saint Paul Quad
Contact: Santee State Park, 251 State Park Road, Santee, SC 29142, (803) 854-2408

Getting there: (From Columbia, SC, 1 hour; from Charleston, SC, 1 hour) At Exit 98 on I-95 at Santee, SC, drive west on Route 6 for 1.2 miles and turn right onto State Park Road (Orangeburg County S-38-105). At the stop sign turn right onto Cleveland Road and go to the south trailhead at the main picnic area.

The Limestone Nature Trail is one of three loop hikes for hikers and their dogs to enjoy in Santee State Park, one of the most popular state parks in South Carolina (for more about the park, see Hike 47). This simple 0.8-mile hike, located in the southeastern corner of the park, is an off-shoot of the longer and moderately difficult Bike/Hike Trail (Hike 48), and begins opposite the entrance to the main picnic area, on the south side of Cleveland Road.

From the parking area, hike counterclockwise, heading west around an arm of Lake Marion, then turn southeast and begin to loop back across a

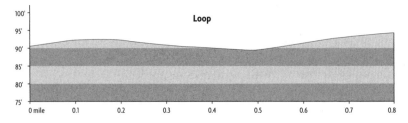

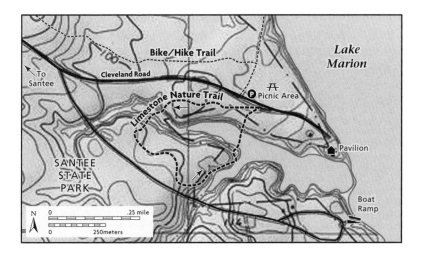

short, rickety bridge, only a short distance from the trailhead. The Limestone Nature Trail is easy and well suited for older or smaller dogs that enjoy a leisurely stroll through the wilderness. Keep your pet on a leash, however, since there are alligators in the Santee State Park—which means the pooch should also stay out of the water. The park service recommends that you carry drinking water and insect repellent in the hot and humid summer months. Hikers can fill up on water at the park visitor center,

Cabins on Lake Marion just west of the visitor center at Santee State Park

located in the northwestern corner of the park (see Hike 47).

For those who would like to make this an overnight adventure, there are 158 campsites and thirty cabins in the park, although dogs are not permitted in or around the cabins.

50. Jarvis Creek Park

Round trip: 1.1 miles
Difficulty: Easy
Hiking time: 30 minutes
High point: 14 feet
Elevation gain: 0 feet
Best season: Any season
Map: USGS Hilton Head Quad
Contact: The Town of Hilton Head Island, One Town Center Court, Hilton Head Island, SC 29928, (843) 341-4600

Getting there: (From Columbia, SC, 3 hours; from Savannah, GA, 45 minutes) On I-95 just north of Hardeeville, SC, take Exit 8 and head east on US 278 for 20.5 miles. Cross the main bridge onto the island over the scenic Intracoastal Waterway, then continue past the ramp to the Cross Island Parkway (US 278), staying on US 278 Business (locally known as the William Hilton Parkway). Just past this intersection, the William Hilton Parkway meets Gum Tree Road and another ramp to the right that leads to the Cross Island Parkway. Continue on the William Hilton Parkway for about 0.2 mile. Jarvis Creek Park is on your right just past Gum Tree Road.

Many people with dogs flock to the Town of Hilton Head Island for a vacation, and most have likely searched for recreational activities for their pets during the visit. Unfortunately, animals are not permitted on the beach during peak hours from Memorial Day to Labor Day, and the trails at the nearby Pickney Wildlife Refuge are off-limits to dogs year-round. The Town

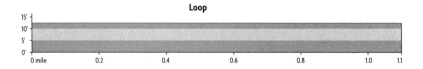

Alec Sedki walks his dog Bishop, a French mastiff, across a boardwalk at Jarvis Creek Park.

of Hilton Head Island came to the rescue, however, with the creation of Jarvis Creek Park, dedicated on May 5, 2003. The $1 million Jarvis Creek Park is part of a rainwater management system for the island that pumps runoff into the freshwater pond for sediment to settle. It is then filtered through the wetlands before being released into Jarvis Creek.

Although US 278 borders the park to the northwest, the trail is very pleasant with a variety of birds frequently visiting the area and wading along the shallow shores of the lake. The Town of Hilton Head was able to protect many of the large oaks and pines in the area, and Jarvis Creek Park offers a surprising amount of solitude on an island that has a tremendous amount of activity.

This loop hike can be completed in either direction, but is profiled here running clockwise. Both hikers and their dogs can enjoy some views of the lake from a floating dock, located near the trailhead. The 53-acre Jarvis Creek Park also includes rest rooms, a public source for drinking water, barbecue grills, a playground, a picnic pavilion, and boardwalks that traverse the wetlands. The asphalt and mulch hiking trails are well marked and easily followed. Dogs are permitted as long as they are kept

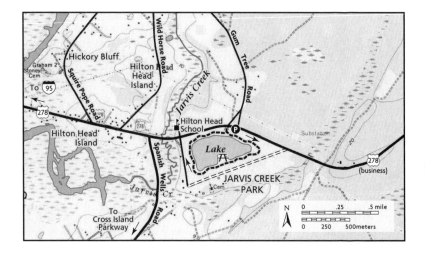

on a leash, and your best option (and the best scenery) is along the main asphalt trail that circumvents the scenic 11-acre lake, stocked with bluegill and largemouth bass for catch-and-release fishing. Keep in mind that the asphalt trail connects to part of the town's 50 miles of multi-use paths, so don't be surprised to see a few slow-moving bicyclists circle the lake as they tour the island.

51. Hunting Island Trail

Round trip: 6 miles
Difficulty: Easy
Hiking time: 3 hours
High point: 10 feet
Elevation gain: Negligible
Best season: Any season
Maps: Hunting Island State Park; USGS Fripp Inlet Quad
Contact: Hunting Island State Park, 2555 Sea Island Parkway, Hunting Island, SC 29920, (843) 838-2011

Getting there: (From Hilton Head, SC, 1 hour; from Charleston, SC, 1.5 hours) At I-95 in Point South, SC, take US 21 east toward Beaufort. Drive 42 miles to where US 21 ends, at Hunting Island State Park. The park entrance is on the left. Follow signs to the visitor center.

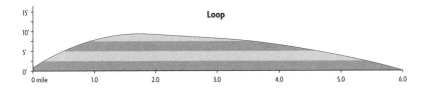

Hunting Island is located a short distance from the popular tourist destination of Hilton Head Island, and is managed as a 5000-acre nature preserve run by South Carolina State Parks. A nineteenth-century lighthouse is on the northern side of the island, with excellent views of both the park and the Atlantic Ocean to the east.

Game hunters named the island and used the maritime forest to track deer, raccoon, birds, and other small game that thrive in the varied habitats of the park. Today, Hunting Island is off-limits to hunters and is a protected preserve where hikers, mountain bikers, and fishermen can enjoy the maritime forests, sandy beaches, and saltwater marshes of the park. There are four separate trails here, and most are a mile or less in length, except for the Island Trail, a 6-mile loop that hugs the southern end of Hunting Island. The Island Trail is marked with brown stakes, and has two small spur trails that lead to the saltwater marsh area to the west.

Begin hiking the Island Trail at Parking Area J, located on the eastern side of the park, and head south along the northern tip of the lagoon, with occasional views over to the cabins run by the state park. After about 2 miles, you'll see a pedestrian bridge crossing the lagoon to the left (east), which connects the cabins to the main trail.

Continue south on the Island Trail, along flat and easy terrain. The ground here is made of sand, mud and roots, but watch out for the occasional crushed oyster shell, which is not always gentle on the pooch's feet. Take some fresh water and insect repellent on the hike—particularly in the summer months. Water is available at the visitor center, just past the main gate.

After the pedestrian bridge, the Island Trail begins a hairpin turn around the southern tip of the island, then turns back to the north. At this turn, a short spur trail leads 1100 feet to a fishing pier that at 1132 feet was once the longest free-standing structure on the East Coast (a pier in Myrtle Beach, South Carolina, now claims the title). Nonetheless, it has outstanding views to the south, and the pooch will likely enjoy the interesting smells typically found around a saltwater pier.

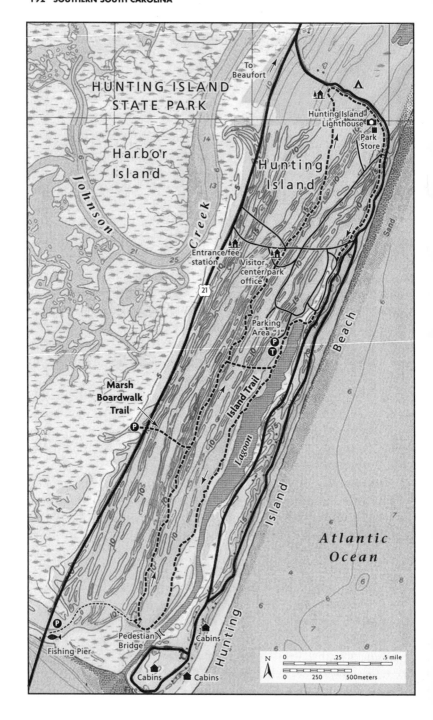

HUNTING ISLAND
STATE PARK

To
Beaufort

Harbor
Island

Hunting Island
Lighthouse

Park
Store

Johnson

Creek

Hunting

Island

Entrance/fee
station

21

Visitor
center/park
office

Parking
Area "J"

Sand

Marsh
Boardwalk
Trail

Island Trail

Beach

Lagoon

Island

Atlantic
Ocean

Hunting

Fishing Pier

Pedestian
Bridge

Cabins

Cabins

Cabins

N

0   .25   .5 mile

0   250   500 meters

The lighthouse at Hunting Island, along the South Carolina coast

From here, it is 2.3 miles to the visitor center on the Island Trail. Continue hiking north and within a mile notice the Marsh Boardwalk Trail on the left. It is a nationally recognized nature and observation trail, and it is a worthy side hike if your dog is still full of energy. Otherwise, continue heading north to the visitor center, which you reach after 4.4 miles on the Island Trail.

Here you have the option of following the road back to Parking Area J (by turning back to the south), or you may walk to the beach and follow it back to Parking Area J.

Remember that the Island Trail is also open to mountain bikers. So keep the pooch on a leash, be courteous, and step off the trail if you see a biker coming.

Although there is no camping permitted in the backcountry or on the beach, Hunting Island State Park does have 200 campsites (which allow dogs) and fourteen vacation cabins (which do not allow dogs). There are also full-service facilities a short distance away in Beaufort.

52. I'on Swamp

Round trip: 2 miles
Difficulty: Easy
Hiking time: 1 hour
High point: 7 feet
Elevation gain: Negligible
Best season: Spring, fall, winter
Map: USGS Ocean Bay Quad
Contact: Wambaw Ranger District, P.O. Box 788, McClellanville, SC
   29458, (843) 887-3257

Getting there: (From Charleston, SC, 1 hour) In Charleston, take US 17 north for 15 miles to I'on Swamp Road (Forest Road 228). Turn left and drive 2 miles to the trailhead, also on the left. The Environmental Education Center has maps and trail information and is located on US 17 just north of Forest Road 228.

This easy loop hike is an interpretive trail through the coastal wetlands of South Carolina. The self-guided tour is lined with interpretive signs that mark an interesting system of canals that were once used by slaves in the 1700s to harvest and transport rice that was grown in the nearby plantation fields. The I'on Swamp Trail parallels these canals and is now a haven for wildlife. There are numerous wooden bird boxes placed throughout the wetlands that support a wide variety of bird species including the wood duck, the warbler, and the blue heron. Hikers may also notice numerous snakes, turtles, and alligators that cruise the drainages next to the trail.

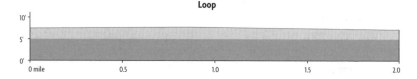

The Witheywood Canal is one of the water-filled canals in the I'on Swamp.

The hike begins at a small parking area on Forest Road 228, known locally as I'on Swamp Road. From here, the white-blazed route follows a short spur trail heading west on an old road to a loop that circles the now abandoned and overgrown rice fields. At the loop, turn left to hike this trail in a clockwise direction, and follow the Witheywood Canal for a short distance through a forest of young hardwoods.

After about a mile, the trail crosses a small canal and makes a hard turn to the northwest. A large alligator calls this area home, and a sign warns of its presence. Make sure to have your dog on a leash as you make the turn—especially with smaller pets, which occasionally make easy targets for these large reptiles.

Hiking northwest, you'll now have the canal on your right for a few hundred yards. The I'on Swamp Trail then turns back to the east and eventually loops around to the spur trail that returns to the parking area at I'on Swamp Road.

This loop hike is best done from the late fall through the early spring.

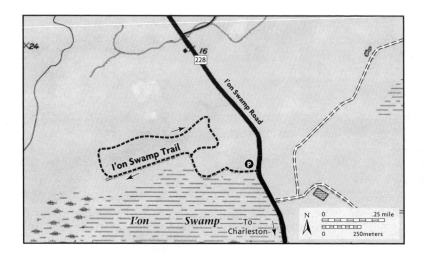

Summers are very hot and humid in the Charleston area, and the insects are quite aggressive (particularly in the evenings), so take insect repellent when hiking at this time of year. Both hikers and their hounds will enjoy the wildlife, and the trail is well marked and easy to follow. Keep in mind, however, that the I'on Swamp is a day-use facility and there are no camping facilities in the forest.

53. Sewee Shell Mound

Round trip: 1 mile
Difficulty: Easy
Hiking time: 30 minutes
High point: 20 feet
Elevation gain: Negligible
Best season: Fall, winter, spring
Map: USGS Sewee Bay Quad
Contact: Sewee Visitor and Environmental Education Center, 5821
U.S. Highway 17 North, Awendaw, SC 29429, (843) 928-3368

Getting there: (From Columbia, SC, 2 hours; from Charleston, SC, 15 minutes) In Charleston, take US 17 north to Doar Road North (Route 432). Turn right and continue 2.5 miles to Salt Pond Road. Turn right on Salt Pond Road and drive 0.5 mile to the trailhead.

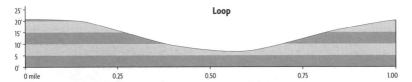

The Sewee Shell Mound hike is a 1-mile, self-guided loop trail tucked along the coast of South Carolina. The interpretive trail is unique in that it consists of a clamshell mound and an oyster ring mound that date back 4000 years to when Native Americans inhabited the area and used what is now the Intracoastal Waterway to catch and harvest their seafood. The mounds are the remnants of a once flourishing community that built its homes along heaps of discarded oyster and clamshells. Archaeologists speculate that the mounds may have been used for ceremonial purposes, and modern-day adventurers can see these ancient formations along the tidal creeks near the Intracoastal Waterway.

The Sewee Shell Mound hike begins at the parking area on the south side of Salt Pond Road. A short spur trail heads south to a loop that has two additional spur trails leading to both the oyster and clam shell mounds. This area was ravaged by Hurricane Hugo in 1989 and by a fire that consumed much of the downed timber a few years later. Surprisingly, the ancient sites and supporting trail system have survived the

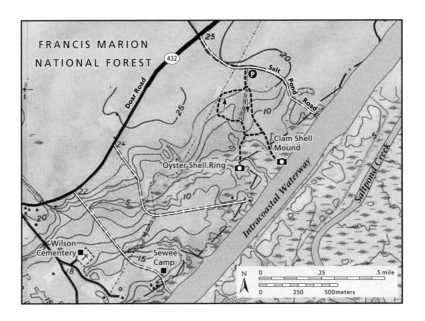

The Oyster Shell Ring, an ancient Indian site along the coast of South Carolina

destruction, and the forest has reclaimed much of the area.

To hike to the shell mounds, leave the parking area and walk to the main loop where you bear left to hike in a clockwise direction. After a short distance, the first spur appears and heads straight out to the clamshell mound, which has excellent views of the Intracoastal Waterway to the east.

In the marshlands around the clamshell mound, you may see several large species of birds, including the osprey, which frequent this area. Dogs may also discover some of the tiny crabs that dwell in small holes along the tidal creeks. During low tide, the ground moves with every step as these tiny creatures scatter and run for cover. Chances are the pooch will be quite excited yet confused about all the ground activity.

From the clamshell ring, backtrack to the main loop and head west to the second spur which leads to the oyster ring. Here along a tidal creek is a white mound of oyster shells that are slowly being consumed by the coastal wilderness. An interpretive sign marks the location, and there are sweeping views to the marshlands that surround the Intracoastal Waterway.

From the oyster ring, backtrack to the main loop and continue back to the parking area where you started.

Like the nearby I'on Swamp Hike (Hike 52), the Sewee Shell Mounds are a day-use facility with no overnight accommodations. There is no potable water source, so bring adequate drinking water.

54. Huntington Beach

Round trip: 9.6 miles
Difficulty: Easy
Hiking time: 2–3 hours
High point: 5 feet
Elevation gain: Negligible
Best season: Any season
Maps: USGS Brookgreen and Magnolia Beach Quads
Contact: Huntington Beach State Park, 16148 Ocean Highway, Murrells Inlet, SC 29576, (843) 237-4440

Getting there: (From Atlanta, GA, 5.5 hours; from Charleston, SC, 1.5 hours) Huntington Beach State Park is located 20 miles north of Georgetown, SC, and 20 miles south of Myrtle Beach, SC. From Myrtle Beach, drive 17 miles on US 17 to Murrells Inlet, then continue another 3 miles south. The park entrance is across from Brookgreen Gardens, on the left. From Georgetown, drive 20 miles northeast on US 17, to the park entrance on the right.

Huntington Beach State Park is named after the American sculptor Anna Hyatt Huntington who used the area as a private beach and studio during the winter months. She and her husband Archer lived in a white Moorish-styled mansion on the south end of the beach and called the site Atalaya. It is now open to the public and is registered as a National Historic Landmark.

This clockwise loop hike starts at the park office and follows Magnolia Beach northeast on a spur trail that ends at a jetty on Oaks Creek. The flat, easy trail is great for older and smaller dogs, and hikers have the

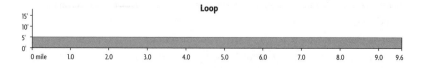

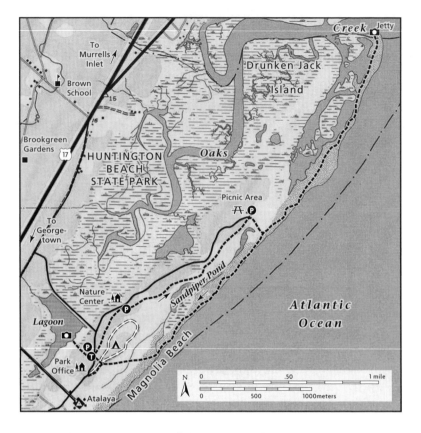

option of cutting 2.6 miles off the route by eliminating the side hike to the Murrells Inlet jetty.

The hike begins at the parking lot for the education center and crosses a boardwalk over black pluff mud and spartina grass through a saltwater marsh. From here, the route follows the trail to Sandpiper Pond and continues northeast, running parallel to the road toward the picnic area, a distance of just over a mile. This section of trail passes through a coastal forest of oak, red cedar, and creeping vines, and there are some observation platforms along the route.

At the picnic area, the trail turns to the coast where hikers can either loop back to the trailhead or follow a spur trail to the jetty. It is a 1.3-mile hike (or 2.6 miles round trip) to the Murrells Inlet jetty where there are outstanding views to the east. Otherwise, turn to the southeast and follow the coast back to the park office and education center.

The pooch will most certainly enjoy the sand and surf at Huntington

The scenic sandy beaches of the South Carolina coast

Beach State Park, but the park service asks that dogs be leashed at all times to protect the rare and endangered birds that nest in the preserve. The area is well known for its habitat, with 2500 acres of undeveloped, pristine nature preserve and over 300 species of birds.

It is critical that the birds not be threatened so that they will return to the area in the future, so please follow the leash guidelines. And be cautious around alligators since they are abundant here and a potential threat for the dog—particularly smaller ones.

There are no backcountry campsites in Huntington Beach State Park, but hikers wishing to stay overnight might enjoy one of the 137 sites at the campground located on the southern end of the park, where drinking water is available for public use.

TRAIL CLUBS

Volunteering is good for you, your pet, and the entire trail system. Not only will you get some exercise and meet new people, but you will also generate goodwill for other dog owners and help to build a trail network that will benefit hikers for years to come. In today's government, competition for wilderness funding is more challenging than ever. The professionals who manage our wild lands are being asked to do more with less and often lack the necessary resources to manage our wild places to their standards. If you would like to help maintain a trail in your area, we highly encourage you to contact some of the groups listed below and offer your assistance. A little volunteer work can go a long way, and many of our trails in Georgia and South Carolina depend on it.

Trail Clubs in Georgia and the Carolinas

The Bartram Trail Society
P.O. Box 144
Scaly Mountain, NC 28775
www.ncbartramtrail.org/index.htm

Benton MacKaye Trail Association
P.O. Box 53271
Atlanta, GA 30355-1271
www.bmta.org

Foothills Trail Conference
P.O. Box 3041
Greeenville, SC 29602
www.foothillstrail.org

Georgia Appalachian Trail Club
P.O. Box 654
Atlanta, GA 30301
(404) 634-6495
www.georgia-atclub.org

Georgia Pinhoti Trail Association, Inc.
P.O. Box 3101
Rome, GA 30164-3101
(706) 766-3800
www.georgiapinhoti.org

Palmetto Conservation Foundation
1314 Lincoln St., Suite 305
Columbia, SC 29201
(803) 771-0870
www.palmettoconservation.org

INDEX

ABOUT THE AUTHORS

Steve "BirdShooter" Goodrich and his wife Ashley live in Atlanta, Georgia, and hike frequently in the southeastern United States. The couple were engaged at Springer Mountain, the terminus of the Appalachian Trail in North Georgia, where Steve began (and eventually completed) a 2144-mile thru-hike in 1994. Although they own and operate a number of outdoor adventure websites, this is their first published work, which shares fifty-four of over 300 hikes they have done in the Southeast with their yellow Lab, Rebel. For additional hikes, trail photos, and biographies of their trail buddies and hounds, visit www.n2backpacking.com.

The authors at the summit of Springer Mountain in North Georgia

THE MOUNTAINEERS, founded in 1906, is a nonprofit outdoor activity and conservation club, whose mission is "to explore, study, preserve, and enjoy the natural beauty of the outdoors...." Based in Seattle, Washington, the club is now the third-largest such organization in the United States, with seven branches throughout Washington State.

The Mountaineers sponsors both classes and year-round outdoor activities in the Pacific Northwest, which include hiking, mountain climbing, ski-touring, snowshoeing, bicycling, camping, kayaking, nature study, sailing, and adventure travel. The club's conservation division supports environmental causes through educational activities, sponsoring legislation, and presenting informational programs.

All club activities are led by skilled, experienced instructors, who are dedicated to promoting safe and responsible enjoyment and preservation of the outdoors.

If you would like to participate in these organized outdoor activities or the club's programs, consider a membership in The Mountaineers. For information and an application, write or call The Mountaineers, Club Headquarters, 300 Third Avenue West, Seattle, WA 98119; 206-284-6310. You can also visit the club's website at www.mountaineers.org or contact The Mountaineers via email at clubmail@mountaineers.org.

The Mountaineers Books, an active, nonprofit publishing program of the club, produces guidebooks, instructional texts, historical works, natural history guides, and works on environmental conservation. All books produced by The Mountaineers Books fulfill the club's mission.

Send or call for our catalog of more than 500 outdoor titles:

The Mountaineers Books
1001 SW Klickitat Way, Suite 201
Seattle, WA 98134
800-553-4453
mbooks@mountaineersbooks.org
www.mountaineersbooks.org

The Mountaineers Books is proud to be a corporate sponsor of The Leave No Trace Center for Outdoor Ethics, whose mission is to promote and inspire responsible outdoor recreation through education, research, and partnerships. The Leave No Trace program is focused specifically on human-powered (nonmotorized) recreation.

Leave No Trace strives to educate visitors about the nature of their recreational impacts, as well as offer techniques to prevent and minimize such impacts. Leave No Trace is best understood as an educational and ethical program, not as a set of rules and regulations.

For more information, visit www.LNT.org, or call 800-332-4100.

OTHER TITLES YOU MIGHT ENJOY FROM
THE MOUNTAINEERS BOOKS

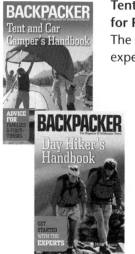
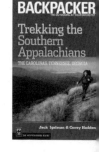

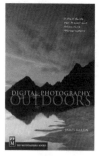